15-minute
GLUTEN-FREE COOKBOOK
for beginners

Quick, Easy Recipes to Cut Gluten, Stay Healthy, and Boost Mental Clarity.

Tips and Food List to Plan Tasty and Sustainable Meals.

Sharon Greenstock

"15-Minute Gluten-Free Cookbook" © Sharon Greenstock - 2024 - **All rights reserved**

All rights reserved. No part of this publication may be reproduced or transmitted in any form or by any means, electronic or mechanical, including photocopying, recording, or by any information storage and retrieval system, without the written permission of the author or the publisher, except permitted by law.

Legal Notice:

The purpose of this work is educational and for personal entertainment only. It is strictly prohibited to copy, use, or disseminate any part of this book, either in its entirety or in part, in any form or manner, without explicit written consent from the author or the publisher.

Disclaimer Notice:

The author and publisher have made every effort to ensure the accuracy of the information herein. However, the author is not responsible for any errors or omissions, or for any actions taken by readers based on the information provided in this book. The content of this book should not be construed as medical, financial, nutritional or legal advice, and readers are advised to seek professional guidance in these areas when necessary.

Table of Contents

INTRODUCTION 7
    Understanding Gluten-Free Living 7
    Transitioning to a GF Lifestyle: #10 Key Strategies 7
Getting Started 9
    Essential Ingredients for a GF Pantry 9
    Finding Gluten-Free Substitutes 10
    Food Science Explanations about Different Flours and Starches 12
CHAPTER 1. POWER-UP RECIPES 14

BREAKFASTS 14	Quinoa and Black Bean Salad 16
Quinoa Breakfast Bowl 14	Mediterranean Tabbouleh 17
Greek Yogurt with Honey and Nuts 15	Black Bean Burgers 17
Avocado Toast 15	Thai Peanut Noodles 17
Oatmeal with Fresh Berries 15	**TASTY SNACKS & BITES** 18
Protein-Packed Peanut Butter Banana Smoothie 15	Hummus and Veggie Platter 18
MAIN DISHES & CRISP SALADS 16	Almond Butter Energy Bites 18
Greek Salad 16	Spiced Nuts 18

CHAPTER 2. DIGESTIVE-FRIENDLY DISHES 19

SOUPS & GREENS DELIGHT 19	Cauliflower Rice 21
Quick Tomato Basil Soup 19	Kale Chips 21
Creamy Carrot Ginger Soup 20	Roasted Brussels Sprouts 21
Caprese Salad 20	Avocado and Chickpea Salad 22
Spinach and Strawberry Salad 20	Baked Sweet Potato Fries 22
SIDES & SNACKS 21	Grilled Asparagus 22

Roasted Chickpeas 22

LIGHT MAIN DISHES 23

Stuffed Bell Peppers 23

Mushroom and Spinach Polenta 23

Italian Zucchini Noodles with Pesto 24

Vietnamese Spring Rolls 24

Egg-Free Veggie Rice Paper Rolls 24

Vegan Buddha Bowl 25

Thai Mango Salad 25

Chickpea and Spinach Curry 25

Vegan Tacos 26

Lebanese Tzatziki with Pita Chips 26

CHAPTER 3. MEALS FOR MENTAL CLARITY 27

SMOOTHIES & BREAKFASTS 27

Smoky BBQ Tofu 27

Green Detox Smoothie 28

Berry Blast Smoothie 28

Almond Flour Pancakes 28

MAIN DISHES 28

Lemon Garlic Salmon 29

Grilled Chicken Caesar Salad 29

Greek Feta Stuffed Mini Peppers 30

Honey Glazed Shrimp 30

Quinoa Pilaf 30

BRAIN-BOOSTING SNACKS & BITES 31

Cucumber and Smoked Salmon Bites 31

Veggie Sushi Rolls 31

Garlic Parmesan Popcorn 31

Avocado Salsa.. 32

Mini Bell Pepper Nachos 32

Spicy Tuna Stuffed Cucumber Cups 32

CHAPTER 4. BALANCED DAILY DISHES 33

SOUP & STEW 33

Sweet Corn Chowder 33

Butternut Squash Soup 33

Chicken and Vegetable Soup 34

Lentil Soup 34

Kale Caesar Salad Errore. Il segnalibro non è definito.

VEGETARIAN AND VEGAN MAIN DISHES 35

Cauliflower Steaks 35

Lentil Shepherd's Pie 35

Mushroom Stir-Fry 36

Vegan Chili 36

Vegan Alfredo Pasta 36

FISH AND POULTRY MAIN DISHES 37

Baked Cod with Herbs 37

Grilled Tilapia Tacos 37

Chicken Stir-Fry 38

Tuna Salad Lettuce Wraps 38

Thai Coconut Chicken 39

Baked Herb Chicken Breasts 39

Turkey Meatballs 40

Chicken Fajitas 40

Quick Shrimp Stir-Fry 41

Lemon Herb Baked Tilapia 41

BEEF AND PORK MAIN DISHES 42

Beef and Broccoli Stir-Fry 42

Gluten-Free Meatloaf..................................42

Spaghetti Bolognese 43

Beef Tacos 43

Pork Stir-Fry..44

Grilled Pork Chops 44

Sausage and Peppers................................45

Quick Beef Stir-Fry 45

Peppered Pork Tenderloin 45

EGGS AND DAIRY-FREE OPTIONS 46

Tofu Scramble 46

Vegan Banana Pancakes.........................46

Chickpea Omelette 47

Dairy-Free Mac and Cheese 47

Coconut Curry Chicken 48

Egg-Free Banana Pancakes.....................48

Tomato Basil Bruschetta 49

Egg-Free Quinoa and Veggie Stir-Fry 49

Egg-Free Veggie Wrap 49

GLOBAL FLAVORS...50

Mexican Quinoa Salad 50

Thai Basil Chicken 50

Japanese Miso Soup 51

Korean Beef Bowl.....................................51

Greek Lemon Garlic Chicken Skewers......52

Moroccan Chickpea Soup 52

Spanish Paella with Seafood....................53

Japanese Miso Soup 53

Mexican Guacamole Tostadas 53

Japanese Edamame and Seaweed Salad...54

Indian Masala Chickpea Wrap..................54

Thai Spring Rolls 54

Egg-Free Fruit and Nut Parfait 54

Italian Caponata Crostini 55

Moroccan Carrot Salad............................55

SNACKS AND APPETIZERS 56

Roasted Chickpeas 56

Kale Chips 56

Crackers with Cheese Spread.................56

Garlic Mashed Potatoes...........................57

Stuffed Dates 57

Deviled Avocado Eggs (Egg-Free Version)58

Zucchini Fritters 58

Cheesy Spinach Dip 59

Apple and Almond Butter Sandwiches 59

Turkey and Veggie Roll-Ups.....................59

DESSERTS AND SWEET TREATS 60

Chocolate Avocado Mousse 60

Coconut Milk Ice Cream 60

Dairy-Free Cheesecake Bites 61

Fruit Sorbet..61

Almond Butter Cookies 61

Lemon Bars 62

Coconut Macaroons.................................62

Quick Peanut Butter Cookies 63

Flourless Chocolate Cake 63

Almond Flour Biscuits..............................64

Cornbread Muffins 64

SAUCES, DRESSINGS, AND STAPLES..............65

Peanut Sauce...65

Pesto Sauce 65

Teriyaki Sauce..66

Balsamic Vinaigrette................................66

Caesar Dressing 66

Chimichurri Sauce...................................67

Ranch Dressing...............................68	**Quick Marinara Sauce**...............................68

FOOD LIST 69

Tips to Plan Sustainable Meals 70

    Quick Prep Strategies for Weeknight Dinners... 70

    Planning for Success: How to Make Time-Saving a Habit 71

Supplementary Contents 72

INTRODUCTION

Understanding Gluten-Free Living

The decision to adopt a gluten-free diet can arise from various needs, whether due to celiac disease, gluten sensitivity, or personal health preferences. Eliminating gluten—a protein found in wheat, barley, and rye—can lead to significant health benefits for those sensitive or allergic to it. For others, it's a lifestyle choice that can lead to improved health outcomes, such as **better digestive health, reduced chronic inflammation, enhanced energy levels but also reduction in Chronic Inflammation, boost mental clarity and an overall better weight management**.

This book is designed for anyone who seeks to simplify their cooking routine while maintaining a gluten-free diet. The recipes within these pages cater to all, from beginners in the kitchen to seasoned cooks looking for quick and easy options. Each recipe is crafted to ensure that you spend little time preparing a meal, from start to finish. What's Inside?

- **Quick and Simple Recipes:** The most part of recipes in this book takes 15 minutes or less to prepare. This quick turnaround does not only cater to the fast-paced lifestyle of modern individuals and families but also ensures that you can enjoy a home-cooked meal without the usual hours spent in the kitchen.
- **Ingredients at Your Fingertips:** We emphasize using common, easily accessible ingredients, which means you won't need to hunt through specialty food stores for rare items. This accessibility is key to sticking with a gluten-free diet without feeling constrained or isolated by your food choices.
- **Health Benefits Galore:** Each recipe is not only designed to be gluten-free but also focuses on overall nutritional value, ensuring that you consume low-fat, health-conscious meals that support a well-rounded diet.
- **Budget-Conscious Meals:** The recipes are created with budget in mind, utilizing ingredients that won't break the bank and techniques that save on energy costs, without sacrificing flavor or quality.

Transitioning to a GF Lifestyle: #10 Key Strategies

Transitioning to a gluten-free lifestyle can be a significant change, especially if you are accustomed to a diet that includes a lot of gluten-containing foods like bread, pasta, and cereals. However, with the right approach and mindset, adopting this new way of eating can become not only manageable but also enjoyable. Let's delve into the Key Strategies:

1. Educate Yourself About Gluten

Learn what gluten is and where it's found, including hidden sources. Understand why it's harmful for those with celiac disease or gluten sensitivity. Study food labels and ingredient lists to identify gluten-containing items to prevents accidental ingestion and ensures informed dietary choices.

2. Plan Your Meals

Plan a week's worth of meals and snacks to avoid last-minute, potentially unhealthy choices. Focus on naturally gluten-free foods and explore new recipes using alternative grains and flours. Consider batch cooking and freezing meals for busy days.

3. Purge and Restock Your Pantry

Clear your kitchen of gluten-containing products and thoroughly clean to avoid cross-contamination. Restock with gluten-free items, always checking labels and ingredient lists. Invest in gluten-free grains, flours, and other staples to expand your cooking options.

4. Learn to Cook and Bake Gluten-Free

Master gluten-free cooking and baking to maintain a satisfying diet. Start with simple recipes and gradually tackle more complex dishes. Experiment with different gluten-free flours and starches to find what works best for various recipes.

5. Communicate Your Needs

Clearly explain your gluten-free requirements when eating out or at others' homes. Most restaurants offer gluten-free options or can modify dishes. When in doubt, choose simple meals with less risk of contamination. When dining with friends or family, offer to bring a safe dish.

6. Find Support

Join local or online gluten-free communities. Share experiences, get advice, and discover new recipes and gluten-free friendly restaurants.

7. Focus on Whole, Naturally Gluten-Free Foods

Base diet on naturally gluten-free foods: fruits, vegetables, meats, fish, dairy, nuts, and legumes. Ensure balanced nutrition.

8. Be Prepared for Emotional Challenges

Acknowledge frustration or deprivation. Find coping strategies. Remember diet reasons. Celebrate victories with non-food rewards.

9. Keep Learning and Adapting

Stay informed about new gluten-free products and recipes. The market evolves, offering more options to improve your diet.

10. Monitor Your Health

Track body's response to gluten-free diet. Regular check-ups for celiac or sensitivity. Observe symptom changes to tailor diet.

Transitioning to a gluten-free lifestyle is a journey that requires patience, dedication, and creativity. By embracing these tips and continuing to educate yourself, you can make the transition smoother and more successful, leading to a healthier and more satisfying way of life.

Getting Started

Essential Ingredients for a GF Pantry

The kitchen is the starting point for a gluten-free lifestyle. While initially challenging, stocking a gluten-free pantry with essential ingredients is key to preparing nutritious and tasty meals. This chapter guides you through the necessary items to keep on hand, enabling you to confidently follow the cookbook's recipes. A well-stocked pantry forms the foundation for successful gluten-free cooking and baking.

1. Gluten-Free Grains and Flours

- **Rice:** A versatile grain that is naturally gluten-free. Keep both white and brown rice for their different textures and nutritional profiles.
- **Quinoa:** High in protein and fiber, quinoa is excellent in salads or as a side dish.
- **Cornmeal:** Perfect for making gluten-free cornbread or as a breading alternative.
- **Buckwheat:** Despite its name, buckwheat is gluten-free and works well for pancakes and noodles.
- **Gluten-Free All-Purpose Flour:** A must-have for baking, look for blends that can be used as a one-to-one substitute for wheat flour.
- **Almond Flour:** Great for baking and breading, it adds a rich, nutty flavor to recipes.
- **Coconut Flour:** Highly absorbent and good for baking, use it to add fiber and texture to dishes.
- **Oat Flour:** Make sure it's labeled gluten-free, as oats can be contaminated with gluten. It's excellent for baking.

Stocking these grains and flours will ensure you can handle most recipes, from baking bread to thickening sauces.

2. Starches and Thickeners

- **Cornstarch:** A fine, powdery starch that is excellent for thickening sauces, gravies, and soups.
- **Potato Starch:** Not to be confused with potato flour, this starch is a wonderful thickener and adds moisture to baked goods.
- **Tapioca Starch:** Derived from cassava, it helps create a chewy texture in baked goods and is also good for thickening.
- **Arrowroot Powder:** A versatile, neutral-tasting thickener for gravies and baking.

3. Pastas and Noodles

- **Rice Noodles:** Ideal for Asian dishes like stir-fries and soups.
- **Corn Pasta:** Offers a similar consistency to traditional pasta and is good in Italian recipes.

- **Quinoa Pasta:** High in protein and has a firm texture, making it suitable for many dishes.
- **Legume-based Pastas:** Made from beans, lentils, or chickpeas, these are nutritious and high in protein.

4. Breads and Cereals

- **Gluten-Free Bread:** Look for whole-grain options without added sugars.
- **Gluten-Free Cereals:** Choose cereals that are low in sugar and high in fiber, such as those made from rice, corn, or quinoa.

5. Baking Additives and Sweeteners

- **Xanthan Gum or Guar Gum:** These are used to replace gluten's elasticity in recipes.
- **Pure Vanilla Extract:** Adds flavor to baked goods.
- **Honey, Maple Syrup, and Agave Nectar:** Natural sweeteners that can be used in baking and beverages.

6. Condiments, Sauces, and Spices

Many sauces and condiments can contain hidden gluten, so it is important to read labels carefully:

- **Tamari:** A gluten-free alternative to soy sauce.
- **Mustard:** Most are gluten-free, but check the label to be sure.
- **Spices and Herbs:** Always check that they are pure and not blends that could contain gluten as a filler.

7. Snacks

- **Nuts and Seeds:** Natural and filling, they are great for snacking or adding to dishes.
- **Popcorn:** A whole grain that's naturally gluten-free.
- **Dried Fruit:** Make sure it's not processed on equipment that handles gluten-containing items.

8. Dairy and Refrigerated Goods

- **Cheese:** Most natural cheeses are gluten-free, but check labels for added starches or flavorings.
- **Yogurt:** Opt for plain varieties without added flavors or granola.
- **Eggs:** A versatile, protein-rich staple that's inherently gluten-free.

A well-stocked gluten-free pantry enables recipe success, culinary flexibility, and new taste discoveries.

Finding Gluten-Free Substitutes

Thanks to the increasing awareness of gluten-related health issues, there are now more substitutes than ever before that can help you enjoy the flavors you love without the gluten. As follows a detailed guidance on finding suitable gluten-free substitutes for common ingredients:

1. Flour Substitutes

- **Gluten-Free All-Purpose Flour:** These blends are designed to mimic the properties of wheat flour and can often be used in a one-to-one ratio. They typically combine several flours and starches like rice flour, tapioca flour, potato starch, and sometimes xanthan gum or guar gum to improve texture.

- **Almond Flour:** Made from finely ground almonds, this flour adds richness and is excellent for baking. It's particularly good in cakes and cookies.
- **Coconut Flour:** Highly absorbent and a little goes a long way. It's great for adding moisture to baked goods but requires more liquid than other flours.
- **Oat Flour:** Ensure it is certified gluten-free. Oat flour has a mild flavor and is fantastic for making bread and other baked items.
- **Chickpea Flour:** Also known as besan or gram flour, it's high in protein and fiber and works well in savory dishes like pancakes or as a binder in fritters.

2. Pasta and Noodle Substitutes

- **Rice Pasta:** Has a neutral flavor and smooth texture, making it a versatile substitute for traditional pasta.
- **Corn Pasta:** Offers a consistency very similar to regular pasta and holds up well in robust sauces.
- **Quinoa Pasta:** Combines the nutritional benefits of quinoa with the familiar form of pasta.
- **Legume-based Pastas:** Made from beans, lentils, or chickpeas, these are not only gluten-free but also high in protein and fiber.

3. Bread Substitutes

- **Gluten-Free Bread Loaves:** Available in most supermarkets, these can closely mimic the texture and taste of wheat-based bread.
- **Corn Tortillas:** A great substitute for bread in sandwiches and wraps.
- **Lettuce Wraps:** A fresh and low-calorie alternative to bread, perfect for wraps and burgers.

4. Cereal Substitutes

- **Gluten-Free Oats:** Make sure they are labeled gluten-free to avoid cross-contamination.
- **Puffed Rice or Corn:** These can be used in homemade muesli or eaten as a breakfast cereal with milk or yogurt.
- **Buckwheat and Quinoa Flakes:** Nutrient-rich alternatives that can be used just like oatmeal.

5. Breadcrumbs and Coating Mixes

For recipes that require a crunchy coating, try these substitutes:

- **Gluten-Free Breadcrumbs:** Readily available in stores or easily made at home using gluten-free bread.
- **Crushed Cornflakes or Rice Cereal:** Ensure they are unsweetened and gluten-free. These can give a satisfying crunch to baked or fried foods.
- **Almond Meal:** Provides a deliciously nutty flavor to dishes, perfect for coating meat or vegetables.

6. Soy Sauce and Condiments

- **Tamari:** A gluten-free alternative to soy sauce, ideal for cooking and dipping.
- **Gluten-Free Mustard and Ketchup:** Check labels carefully as some brands may include gluten.
- **Prepared Salad Dressings:** Opt for gluten-free labels or make your own from scratch.

7. Beer and Beverages

Traditional beer contains gluten, but there are gluten-free options:

- **Gluten-Free Beer:** Brewed to remove gluten or made from gluten-free grains.
- **Ciders:** Naturally gluten-free and available in a variety of flavors.

8. Dessert and Sweet Treat Substitutes

- **Gluten-Free Baking Mixes:** For cakes, cookies, and muffins, these mixes are available in most grocery stores.
- **Natural Sweeteners:** Like honey, maple syrup, and agave nectar, these are gluten-free and can add sweetness to any dessert.

Food Science Explanations about Different Flours and Starches

Understanding the science behind gluten-free flours and starches is key to mastering gluten-free cooking and baking. Unlike wheat flour, which contains gluten that forms a network to trap air and provide structure and elasticity, gluten-free flours lack this protein. Therefore, different approaches and combinations are required to mimic these characteristics. This section delves into the properties of various gluten-free flours and starches, explaining how they function and how you can best use them in your cooking.

1. Rice Flour

Properties: one of the most used gluten-free flours due to its neutral flavor and fine texture. It is made from either white or brown rice and acts as a good base for gluten-free flour blends.

How it Works: It is relatively dense and can produce a gritty texture if used alone. It lacks the binding qualities of gluten, so it often requires a starch like tapioca or potato starch to improve the texture of the finished product.

Best Uses: excellent for use in noodles, as a thickening agent in sauces and soups, and in combination with other gluten-free flours for baking breads and pastries.

2. Almond Flour

Properties: made from finely ground almonds, it is rich in protein and naturally GF. It has a moist texture and a buttery flavor, which adds richness to recipes.

How it Works: It is high in fat, which helps to add moisture and tenderness to baked goods. However, because it is so dense and heavy, it's often best when mixed with lighter flours and starches to prevent overly dense results.

Best Uses: Ideal for baking cookies, cakes, and quick breads, or for breading in place of breadcrumbs.

3. Coconut Flour

Properties: made from dried coconut meat and is highly absorbent. It is high in fiber.

How it Works: Due to its high absorbency, a small amount of coconut flour goes a long way, and it requires a lot of moisture, so recipes using coconut flour will often call for extra eggs or liquid.

Best Uses: Works well in pancakes, muffins, and cakes where its absorbency helps to create a soft, tender texture.

4. Tapioca Starch

Properties: Tapioca starch (or tapioca flour) is extracted from the cassava root. It is light, very smooth, and slightly sweet.

How it Works: excellent binder and thickener, contributing a chewy texture and promoting browning in baked goods. It is also great for creating a crisp crust and for thickening sauces without imparting a starchy flavor.

Best Uses: Ideal for pie fillings, puddings, batters, and blends well with other gluten-free flours for bread and pastry recipes.

5. Potato Starch

Properties: it is a fine white powder with neutral taste. It is not to be confused with potato flour, which is made from whole dried potatoes and has a much heavier texture and flavor.

How it Works: Potato starch is excellent for adding moisture to baked goods and is also used as a thickener in soups, sauces, and gravies. It absorbs water effectively and can help extend the shelf life of baked products.

Best Uses: It is commonly used in baking, especially in combination with other gluten-free flours to create light and fluffy cakes and bread.

6. Chickpea Flour

Properties: Also known as gram flour or besan, chickpea flour is made from ground chickpeas and has a slightly earthy flavor. It is high in protein and fiber.

How it Works: Chickpea flour is dense and binding, which makes it a good substitute for eggs in recipes. It's also an excellent thickener and works well in deep-fried coatings and batters.

Best Uses: Great for making flatbreads, fritters, pancakes, and as a binding agent in veggie burgers.

7. Buckwheat Flour

Properties: Despite its name, buckwheat is not related to wheat and is completely gluten-free. It has a strong, nutty flavor and is rich in minerals and antioxidants.

How it Works: Buckwheat flour is heavier than rice flour but lighter than almond or coconut flour, making it a good middle-ground option. It adds robust flavor and color to dishes.

Best Uses: Excellent for making heartier items like soba noodles, pancakes, and artisanal bread.

By understanding the unique properties and best uses of these gluten-free flours and starches, you can begin to experiment more confidently with gluten-free recipes. Mixing and matching these ingredients can help you achieve textures and flavors that are close to their gluten-containing counterparts, enabling you to enjoy a broader range of dishes without compromising on taste or texture.

POWER-UP RECIPES

Fuel your day with recipes designed to support long-lasting energy. These dishes feature nutrient-packed ingredients that keep you energized, reduce fatigue, and sustain you through even the busiest of schedules.

BREAKFASTS

Quinoa Breakfast Bowl

What do you need (Serve 2):

- 1/2 cup cooked quinoa
- 1/4 cup almond milk or any kind of milk
- 1 tablespoon honey or maple syrup
- 1/2 teaspoon cinnamon

Toppings: sliced banana, blueberries, and a sprinkle of chia seeds

How to Proceed:

1. In a bowl, combine the cooked quinoa with almond milk, honey (or maple syrup), and cinnamon.
2. Warm in the microwave for 1-2 minutes until warm.
3. Top with sliced banana, blueberries, and chia seeds.

Nutritional Facts:
Calories: 285 | Protein: 6g | Carbohydrates: 53g | Fat: 5g | Fiber: 5g

Greek Yogurt with Honey and Nuts

What do you need (Serve 1):

- 1 cup plain Greek yogurt
- 2 tablespoons honey
- 1/4 cup mixed nuts, chopped (almonds, walnuts, pecans)

How to Proceed:

1. Place the Greek yogurt in a serving bowl.
2. Drizzle with honey and top with chopped nuts.

Nutritional Facts: Calories: 310 | Protein: 20g | Carbohydrates: 36g | Fat: 10g | Fiber: 2g

Avocado Toast

What do you need (Serve 2):

- 2 slices of GF bread
- 1 ripe avocado
- Salt and pepper to taste

Optional toppings: sliced tomatoes, radishes, or a sprinkle of sesame seeds

How to Proceed:
1. Toast the slices of GF bread until golden and crispy.
2. In a bowl, mash the avocado with a fork and season with salt and pepper.
3. Spread the mashed avocado evenly over the toasted bread.
4. Add any additional toppings as desired.

Nutritional Facts: Calories: 250 | Protein: 5g | Carbohydrates: 27g | Fat: 14g | Fiber: 7g

Oatmeal with Fresh Berries

What do you need (Serve 2):

- 1/2 cup rolled oats
- 1 cup water or milk
- 1/2 cup fresh berries (strawberries, blueberries, raspberries)
- 1 tablespoon honey or maple syrup

How to Proceed:

1. In a saucepan, heat water or milk until it boils.
2. Incorporate the GF oats and bring down to a quite simmer.
3. Cook for 5-7 minutes, stirring occasionally, until the oats are soft.
4. Pour into a bowl and top with fresh berries and a drizzle of honey or maple syrup.

Nutritional Facts: Calories: 210 | Protein: 6g | Carbohydrates: 39g | Fat: 3g | Fiber: 5g

Protein-Packed Peanut Butter Banana Smoothie

What you need (Serve 1):

- 1 ripe banana
- 2 tablespoons peanut butter (unsweetened)
- 1 cup almond milk (or any other plant-based milk)
- 1 tablespoon chia seeds
- 1 tablespoon unsweetened cocoa powder (optional)
- 1 teaspoon honey (optional)
- 3-4 ice cubes

How to Proceed:

1. Place the banana, peanut butter, almond milk, chia seeds, cocoa powder (if using), and honey (if using) into a blender.
2. Blend until smooth and creamy.
3. Add the ice cubes and blend again until the ice is completely crushed.
4. Pour into a glass and serve immediately.

Nutritional Facts:
Calories: 350 | Protein: 10g | Carbohydrates: 40g | Fat: 16g | Fiber: 8g

MAIN DISHES & CRISP SALADS

Greek Salad

What do you need (Serve 2):

- 1 cucumber, diced
- 2 tomatoes, diced
- 1/2 red onion, thinly sliced
- 1/4 cup pitted Kalamata olives
- 1/4 cup crumbled feta cheese
- 2 tbsp olive oil
- 1 tbsp red wine vinegar
- Salt and pepper to taste
- 1/2 tsp dried oregano

How to Proceed:

1. In a bowl, mix cucumber, tomatoes, red onion, and olives.
2. In a small pot, combine olive oil, red wine vinegar, oregano, salt, and pepper.
3. Pour the dressing over the vegetables and toss to coat.
4. Sprinkle feta cheese on top just before serving.
5. Serve chilled.

Nutritional Facts:
Calories: 180 | Protein: 4g | Carbohydrates: 10g | Fat: 15g | Fiber: 2g

Quinoa and Black Bean Salad

What do you need (Serve 2):

- 1 cup cooked quinoa
- 1 cup canned black beans, rinsed and drained
- 1 red bell pepper, diced
- 1/4 cup finely chopped cilantro
- 2 tbsp lime juice
- 1 tbsp olive or vegetable oil
- Salt and pepper to taste

How to Proceed:

1. In a large bowl, combine quinoa, black beans, red bell pepper, and cilantro.
2. In a small bowl, whisk together lime juice, oil, salt, and pepper.
3. Pour the dressing over the quinoa mixture and toss to combine.
4. Chill in the refrigerator before serving to enhance the flavors.

Nutritional Facts:
Calories: 200 | Protein: 8g | Carbohydrates: 30g | Fat: 6g | Fiber: 8g

Mediterranean Tabbouleh

What do you need:

- 1 cup cooked quinoa (cooled)
- 1/2 cup chopped parsley
- 1/4 cup chopped mint
- 1/2 cup diced tomatoes
- 1/4 cup diced cucumber
- 2 tbsp lemon juice
- 2 tbsp olive oil
- Salt and pepper to taste

How to Proceed:
1. In a large bowl, combine cooked quinoa, parsley, mint, tomatoes, and cucumber.
2. Drizzle with lemon juice and olive oil.
3. Season with salt and pepper to taste.
4. Toss gently to combine all ingredients.
5. Serve immediately.

Nutritional Facts: Calories: 180 | Protein: 4g | Carbohydrates: 24g | Fat: 8g | Fiber: 3g

Black Bean Burgers

What do you need (Serve 4):

- 1 can (15 oz) black beans, well-drained and mashed
- 1/2 cup GF breadcrumbs
- 1 teaspoon garlic powder
- 1 teaspoon onion powder
- 1/2 teaspoon smoked paprika
- Salt and pepper to taste
- 2 tablespoons olive oil for frying

How to Proceed:
1. In a bowl, combine mashed black beans, breadcrumbs, garlic powder, onion powder, smoked paprika, salt, and pepper. Combine well.
2. Shape the mixture into patties.
3. Warm up oil in a skillet over medium heat.
4. Cook patties for few minutes on each side until crispy.
5. Serve on GF buns with your favorite toppings.

Nutritional Facts: Calories: 250 | Protein: 8g | Carbohydrates: 33g | Fat: 10g | Fiber: 7g

Thai Peanut Noodles

What do you need (Serve 4):

- 8 oz GF rice noodles
- 1/4 cup natural peanut butter
- 2 tablespoons GF soy sauce or tamari sauce
- 1 tablespoon lime juice
- 1 tablespoon honey or maple syrup
- 1 teaspoon grated ginger
- 1 clove garlic, minced
- 1/4 teaspoon crushed red pepper flakes (optional)
- Chopped green onions and crushed peanuts for garnish

How to Proceed:
1. Cook the rice noodles according to package instructions, then drain and set aside.
2. In a bowl, combine peanut butter, soy sauce, lime juice, honey, ginger, garlic, and red pepper flakes until smooth.
3. Mix the noodles with the peanut sauce until they are thoroughly coated.
4. Serve garnished with chopped green onions and crushed peanuts.

Nutritional Facts: Calories: 320 | Protein: 8g | Carbohydrates: 49g | Fat: 10g | Fiber: 2g

TASTY SNACKS & BITES

Hummus and Veggie Platter

What do you need (Serves 4):

- 1 cup store-bought or homemade hummus
- 1 cucumber, sliced
- 1 bell pepper, sliced
- 1 carrot, peeled and sliced
- 1/4 cup olives
- 1/4 cup cherry tomatoes

How to Proceed:

1. Arrange the hummus in a small bowl in the center of a large plate or serving tray.
1. Neatly arrange the cucumber slices, bell pepper slices, carrot sticks, olives, and cherry tomatoes around the hummus.
2. Serve immediately for fresh, crisp vegetables and smooth, flavorful hummus.

Nutritional Facts:
Calories: 180 | Protein: 5g | Carbohydrates: 20g | Fat: 10g | Fiber: 5g

Almond Butter Energy Bites

What do you need:

- 1/2 cup GF oats
- 1/4 cup almond butter
- 2 tbsp honey or maple syrup
- 2 tbsp chia seeds
- 1/4 tsp vanilla extract
- 1/4 cup mini chocolate chips (optional)

How to Proceed:

1. In a bowl, mix together the oats, almond butter, honey, chia seeds, and vanilla extract.
2. Stir in the mini chocolate chips if using.
3. Roll the mixture into small bite-sized balls.
4. Place in the refrigerator for 10 minutes to set.
5. Serve immediately or store in the refrigerator for later.

Nutritional Facts: Calories: 100 | Protein: 2g | Carbohydrates: 12g | Fat: 5g | Fiber: 2g

Spiced Nuts

What do you need:

- 1 cup mixed nuts (almonds, cashews, walnuts)
- 1 tbsp olive oil
- 1/2 tsp smoked paprika
- 1/4 tsp cumin
- 1/4 tsp garlic powder
- Salt to taste

How to Proceed:

1. Heat olive oil in a skillet over medium heat.
2. Add the mixed nuts and stir to coat with the oil.
3. Sprinkle with smoked paprika, cumin, garlic powder, and salt.
4. Toast the nuts for 5-7 minutes, stirring frequently, until fragrant and lightly browned.
5. Let cool slightly before serving.

Nutritional Facts: Calories: 200 | Protein: 5g | Carbohydrates: 8g | Fat: 18g | Fiber: 3g

DIGESTIVE-FRIENDLY DISHES

These recipes are perfect for easy digestion and reducing bloating. They feature light ingredients like fresh veggies, soothing soups, and fiber-rich dishes that keep you feeling comfortable and satisfied.

SOUPS & GREENS DELIGHT

Quick Tomato Basil Soup

What do you need (Serve 4):

- 2 cups canned crushed tomatoes
- 1 cup hot GF vegetable broth
- 1/4 cup fresh basil, chopped
- 1 garlic clove, minced
- 2 tbsp heavy cream (optional)
- Salt and pepper to taste
- Olive oil for sautéing

How to Proceed:
1. In a medium saucepan, heat a splash of olive oil over medium heat.
2. Add the minced garlic and sauté for about 1 minute until fragrant.
3. Pour in the crushed tomatoes and vegetable broth and bring to a simmer.
4. Add chopped basil, salt, and pepper, and let simmer for about 10 minutes to blend the flavors.
5. Stir in heavy cream if using, heat through for a couple of minutes, and adjust seasoning. Serve hot.

Nutritional Facts: Calories: 150 | Protein: 3g | Carbohydrates: 18g | Fat: 8g | Fiber: 4g

Creamy Carrot Ginger Soup

What do you need (Serve 4):

- 1 lb carrots, peeled and chopped
- 4 cups hot GF vegetable broth
- 1 tbsp fresh ginger, grated
- 1/2 cup coconut milk
- Salt and pepper to taste
- Olive oil for sautéing

How to Proceed:

1. In a pot, warm up a splash of olive oil over medium heat.
2. Add the chopped carrots and grated ginger, and sauté for 5 minutes.
3. Pour in the vegetable broth and bring to a boil.
4. Reduce heat and simmer until carrots are tender, about 10 minutes.
5. Utilize a hand blender to liquefy the soup into a velvety texture.
6. Stir in coconut milk and season with salt and pepper.
7. Heat through for another minute, then serve.

Nutritional Facts:
Calories: 140 | Protein: 2g | Carbohydrates: 18g | Fat: 7g | Fiber: 4g

Caprese Salad

What do you need (Serve 1):

- 2 large ripe tomatoes, sliced
- 1 ball fresh mozzarella cheese, sliced
- Fresh basil leaves
- 2 tbsp olive oil
- 1 tbsp balsamic glaze
- Salt and pepper to taste

How to Proceed:

1. Put the sliced tomatoes and mozzarella cheese alternately on a plate, overlapping them for presentation.
2. Insert basil leaves between the slices.
3. Drizzle with olive oil and balsamic glaze.
4. Season with salt and pepper.
5. Serve immediately.

Nutritional Facts:
Calories: 250 | Protein: 10g | Carbohydrates: 8g | Fat: 20g | Fiber: 2g

Spinach and Strawberry Salad

What do you need (Serve 2):

- 2 cups fresh spinach leaves
- 1 cup sliced strawberries
- 1/4 cup sliced almonds
- 1/4 cup crumbled goat cheese
- 2 tbsp balsamic vinegar
- 1 tbsp olive/vegetable oil
- Salt and pepper to taste

How to Proceed:

1. In a pot, mix the spinach leaves and sliced strawberries.
2. Top with sliced almonds and crumbled goat cheese.
3. In a bowl, mix balsamic vinegar, oil, salt, and pepper.
4. Drizzle the dressing over the salad and toss gently.
5. Serve immediately to ensure freshness and crispness.

Nutritional Facts:
Calories: 180 | Protein: 6g | Carbohydrates: 10g | Fat: 14g | Fiber: 3g

SIDES & SNACKS

Cauliflower Rice

What do you need (Serve 4):

- 1 head cauliflower, grated into small pieces
- 1 tablespoon olive/vegetable oil
- Salt and pepper to taste

How to Proceed:
1. Warm up the oil in a large skillet over medium heat.
2. Incorporate the grated cauliflower and sauté for about 5-8 minutes, until tender and slightly crispy.
3. Season with salt and pepper.
4. Serve warm as a low-carb alternative to rice.

Nutritional Facts:
Calories: 100 | Protein: 4g | Carbohydrates: 10g | Fat: 5g | Fiber: 5g

Kale Chips

What do you need (Serve 2):

- 1 bunch kale, stems removed and leaves torn into bite-sized pieces
- 1 tablespoon olive/vegetable oil
- Salt to taste

How to Proceed:
1. Warm up the oven to 350°F (175°C).
2. Wash and thoroughly dry the kale pieces.
3. Place the kale in a bowl, drizzle with oil, and sprinkle with salt. Toss to coat evenly.
4. Spread the kale on a baking sheet in a single layer.
5. Bake for about 10-12 minutes, or until crisp and the edges are slightly browned. Be careful not to overcook.
6. Serve immediately as a light and crispy snack.

Nutritional Facts: Calories: 60 | Protein: 2g | Carbohydrates: 5g | Fat: 4g | Fiber: 1g

Roasted Brussels Sprouts

What do you need (Serve 4):

- 2 cups Brussels sprouts, halved
- 2 tablespoons olive oil
- Salt and pepper to taste

How to Proceed:
1. Warm up your oven to 400°F (200°C).
2. Toss the Brussels sprouts with oil, salt, and pepper.
3. Spread them out on a baking sheet in a single layer.
4. Cook in the oven for about 12-15 minutes, until crisp on the outside and tender on the inside.
5. Serve hot.

Nutritional Facts: Calories: 120 | Protein: 4g | Carbohydrates: 10g | Fat: 8g | Fiber: 4g

Avocado and Chickpea Salad

What do you need (Serve 4):

- 1 can (15 oz) chickpeas, rinsed and drained
- 1 ripe avocado, diced
- 1/4 cup diced red onion
- 1/4 cup chopped cilantro
- Juice of 1 lime
- 2 tbsp olive/vegetable oil
- Salt and pepper to taste

How to Proceed:

1. In a bowl, combine chickpeas, diced avocado, red onion, and chopped cilantro.
2. In a small bowl, whisk lime juice, oil, salt, and pepper.
3. Pour the dressing over the chickpea mixture and gently toss to combine.
4. Adjust seasoning as needed and chill for about an hour to enrich flavors.

Nutritional Facts:
Calories: 220 | Protein: 7g | Carbohydrates: 23g | Fat: 12g | Fiber: 8g

Baked Sweet Potato Fries

What do you need (Serve 4):

- 2 large sweet potatoes, peeled and cut into strips
- 2 tablespoons olive/vegetable oil
- Salt and pepper to taste

How to Proceed:

1. Warm up your oven to 425°F (220°C).
2. Toss the sweet potato strips with oil, salt, and pepper.
3. Spread them out on a baking sheet in a single layer.
4. Bake for about 12-15 minutes, turning once, until golden and crisp.
5. Serve hot.

Nutritional Facts:
Calories: 180 | Protein: 2g | Carbohydrates: 27g | Fat: 7g | Fiber: 4g

Grilled Asparagus

What do you need (Serve 2):

- 1 bunch asparagus, trimmed
- 2 tablespoons oil
- Salt and pepper to taste
- Lemon wedges for serving

How to Proceed:

1. Warm up your grill to medium-high heat.
2. Toss the asparagus with olive oil, salt, and pepper.
3. Grill the asparagus for about 7-10 minutes, turning occasionally, until charred.
4. Serve hot with lemon wedges.

Nutritional Facts:
Calories: 80 | Protein: 3g | Carbohydrates: 5g | Fat: 6g | Fiber: 2g

Roasted Chickpeas

What do you need (Serve 4):

- 1 can (15 oz) chickpeas, rinsed and drained
- 1 tablespoon olive/vegetable oil
- 1/2 teaspoon smoked paprika
- 1/2 teaspoon garlic powder
- Salt and pepper to taste

How to Proceed:

1. Warm up the oven to 400°F (200°C).
2. Pat the chickpeas dry with paper towels and place them on a baking sheet.
3. Drizzle with olive oil and sprinkle with smoked paprika, garlic powder, salt, and pepper. Toss to coat evenly.
4. Cook in the preheated oven for about 10-15 minutes, or until crispy and golden.
5. Serve warm or at room temperature as a crunchy snack.

Nutritional Facts: Calories: 150 | Protein: 5g | Carbohydrates: 20g | Fat: 5g | Fiber: 6g

LIGHT MAIN DISHES

Stuffed Bell Peppers

What do you need (Serve 4):

- 4 large bell peppers, any color, tops cut off and seeds removed
- 1 cup cooked quinoa
- 1 can (15 oz) black beans, rinsed and drained
- 1 cup corn kernels (fresh or frozen)
- 1/2 cup chopped fresh tomatoes
- 1 teaspoon chili powder
- 1/2 teaspoon cumin
- Salt and pepper to taste
- 1/2 cup shredded vegan cheese (optional)

How to Proceed:

3. In a pot, incorporate quinoa, black beans, corn, tomatoes, chili powder, cumin, salt, and pepper.
4. Stuff the mixture evenly into the hollowed-out bell peppers.
5. Top with vegan cheese if using.
6. Microwave on high for about 5-7 minutes or until the peppers are tender.
7. Serve.

Nutritional Facts:
Calories: 220 | Protein: 8g | Carbohydrates: 40g | Fat: 3g | Fiber: 9g

Mushroom and Spinach Polenta

What do you need:

- 1 cup GF polenta
- 4 cups hot water or vegetable broth
- 1/2 teaspoon salt
- 2 tablespoons olive/vegetable oil
- 1 onion, chopped
- 2 cups sliced mushrooms
- 2 cups fresh spinach
- Salt and pepper to taste
-

How to Proceed:

1. In a saucepan, bring water or vegetable broth to a boil. Gradually whisk in polenta and salt, reduce heat to low, and cook, stirring often, until polenta is thick and creamy, about 10-15 minutes.
2. In another skillet, warm up oil over medium heat. Add onion and mushrooms and cook until softened, about 5-7 minutes.
3. Mix spinach and cook until just wilted, about 2-3 minutes. Season as desired.
4. Serve the mushroom and spinach mixture over the warm polenta.

Nutritional Facts:
Calories: 250 | Protein: 6g | Carbohydrates: 38g | Fat: 9g | Fiber: 4g

Italian Zucchini Noodles with Pesto

What do you need:

- 4 zucchinis, spiralized into noodles
- 1/2 cup GF basil pesto (or homemade pesto)
- 2 tablespoons pine nuts, toasted
- 2 tablespoons olive oil
- Salt and pepper to taste
- Parmesan cheese, grated (optional)

How to Proceed:

1. Warm up oil in a large skillet over medium heat.
2. Mix zucchini noodles and sauté for about 3-5 minutes until tender.
3. Stir in pesto and cook for an additional 2 minutes until heated through.
4. Season with salt and pepper.
5. Serve topped with toasted pine nuts and grated Parmesan cheese if desired.

Nutritional Facts: Calories: 290 | Protein: 6g | Carbohydrates: 8g | Fat: 27g | Fiber: 1g

Vietnamese Spring Rolls

What do you need:

- 8-10 rice paper wrappers
- 1 cup cooked shrimp, halved
- 1 cup vermicelli rice noodles, cooked
- 1 cup thinly sliced cucumber
- 1 cup shredded carrots
- 1 cup fresh mint leaves
- 1 cup fresh cilantro
- Warm water for softening rice papers

For the dipping sauce:
- ✓ 2 tablespoons GF soy sauce
- ✓ 1 tablespoon lime juice
- ✓ 1 teaspoon honey
- ✓ 1/2 teaspoon crushed red pepper flakes

How to Proceed:

1. Fill a large shallow dish with warm water. Dip one rice paper wrapper into the water for about 15-20 seconds until it just becomes pliable.
2. Lay the wrapper flat on a clean, wet surface. On one edge of the wrapper, place a small amount of shrimp, noodles, cucumber, carrots, mint, and cilantro.
3. Roll the wrapper tightly around the filling, folding in the sides as you roll.
4. Repeat with the remaining ingredients.
5. Mix soy sauce, lime juice, honey, and red pepper flakes in a small bowl for the dipping sauce.
6. Serve the spring rolls with the dipping sauce on the side.

Nutritional Facts: Calories: 220 | Protein: 8g | Carbohydrates: 40g | Fat: 2g | Fiber: 1g

Egg-Free Veggie Rice Paper Rolls

What do you need:

- 4 rice paper wrappers
- 1/2 cup thinly sliced bell peppers
- 1/2 cup shredded carrots
- 1/4 cup sliced cucumbers
- 1/4 cup fresh mint leaves
- 1/4 cup fresh cilantro leaves
- 2 tbsp GF tamari or soy sauce for dipping

How to Proceed:

1. Dip each rice paper wrapper in warm water for about 10 seconds to soften.
2. Lay the softened wrapper on a flat surface.
3. Place a small amount of bell peppers, carrots, cucumbers, mint, and cilantro in the center of the wrapper.
4. Fold the sides of the wrapper over the filling, then roll it up tightly.
5. Repeat with the remaining wrappers and ingredients.
6. Serve immediately with GF tamari.

Nutritional Facts: Calories: 100 | Protein: 2g | Carbohydrates: 22g | Fat: 1g | Fiber: 2g

Vegan Buddha Bowl

What do you need (Serve 4):

- 1 cup cooked quinoa
- 1/2 cup chickpeas, rinsed and drained
- 1/2 cup diced cucumbers
- 1/2 cup shredded carrots
- 1/2 cup red cabbage, shredded
- 1/4 cup hummus
- 1 tablespoon sesame seeds
- 2 tablespoons GF lemon tahini dressing

How to Proceed:

1. Arrange quinoa, chickpeas, cucumbers, carrots, and red cabbage in a serving bowl.
2. Top with a dollop of hummus.
3. Drizzle with lemon tahini dressing and sprinkle sesame seeds over the top.
4. Serve immediately, tossing everything together just before eating.

Nutritional Facts: Calories: 320 | Protein: 13g | Carbohydrates: 45g | Fat: 10g | Fiber: 9g

Thai Mango Salad

What do you need:

- 1 ripe mango, julienned
- 1/2 cup julienned carrots
- 1/4 cup chopped cilantro
- 1 tbsp lime juice
- 1 tbsp fish sauce or GF soy sauce
- 1/2 tsp sugar
- 1/4 tsp red chili flakes (optional)

How to Proceed:

1. In a bowl, combine julienned mango, carrots, and chopped cilantro.
2. In a small bowl, mix lime juice, fish sauce (or soy sauce), sugar, and red chili flakes if using.
3. Pour the dressing over the mango salad and toss gently to combine.
4. Serve immediately.

Nutritional Facts: Calories: 110 | Protein: 1g | Carbohydrates: 28g | Fat: 0g | Fiber: 3g

Chickpea and Spinach Curry

What do you need (Serve 4):

- 1 can (15 oz) chickpeas, rinsed and drained
- 2 cups fresh spinach leaves
- 1 cup coconut milk
- 1 tablespoon curry powder
- 1 teaspoon garlic powder
- Salt and pepper to taste
- 2 tablespoons olive oil

How to Proceed:

1. Warm up oil in a skillet over medium heat.
2. Incorporate curry powder and garlic powder, and stir few minutes until fragrant.
3. Incorporate chickpeas and coconut milk, bring to a simmer.
4. Stir in spinach, cover, and cook for about 3-5 minutes until the spinach is wilted and the curry is slightly thickened.
5. Season with salt and pepper.
6. Serve hot, ideally over cooked quinoa or rice.

Nutritional Facts:
Calories: 330 | Protein: 9g | Carbohydrates: 35g | Fat: 18g | Fiber: 9g

Vegan Tacos

What do you need (Serve 4):

- 1 can (15 oz) black beans, rinsed and drained
- 1 cup corn kernels (fresh or frozen)
- 1 avocado, diced
- 1/2 cup chopped fresh cilantro
- Juice of 1 lime
- Salt and pepper to taste
- 4-6 GF corn tortillas

How to Proceed:

1. In a bowl, mix black beans, corn, avocado, cilantro, lime juice, salt, and pepper.
2. Warm up the corn tortillas in a microwave for about 30 seconds or until warm and pliable.
3. Spoon the filling into the tortillas and fold.
4. Serve immediately, optionally with additional lime wedges or salsa.

Nutritional Facts: Calories: 250 | Protein: 9g | Carbohydrates: 37g | Fat: 8g | Fiber: 10g

Lebanese Tzatziki with Pita Chips

What do you need (Serve 4):

- 1 cup dairy-free yogurt (such as coconut or almond yogurt)
- 1/2 cucumber, grated and drained
- 1 clove garlic, minced
- 1 tbsp lemon juice
- 1 tbsp chopped fresh mint or dill
- Salt and pepper to taste
- 4 GF pita bread rounds, cut into triangles
- 1 tbsp olive oil

How to Proceed:

1. Preheat the oven to 350°F (175°C).
2. Arrange the GF pita triangles on a baking sheet. Brush with olive oil and sprinkle with a little salt.
3. Bake for 5-7 minutes until crisp and golden.
4. Meanwhile, in a bowl, combine dairy-free yogurt, grated cucumber, minced garlic, lemon juice, and fresh mint or dill.
5. Season with salt and pepper to taste.
6. Serve the tzatziki with the warm gluten-free pita chips.

Nutritional Facts: Calories: 150 | Protein: 4g | Carbohydrates: 20g | Fat: 7g | Fiber: 2g

MEALS FOR MENTAL CLARITY

These recipes are crafted to support focus and mental sharpness, incorporating nutrient-dense ingredients like leafy greens, berries, nuts, and fatty fish. Rich in omega-3s, antioxidants, and essential B vitamins, they nourish the brain, enhance concentration, and keep you feeling alert throughout the day.

SMOOTHIES & BREAKFASTS

Smoky BBQ Tofu

What do you need:

- 1 block firm tofu, pressed and sliced
- 1/4 cup GF BBQ sauce
- 1 tablespoon olive/vegetable oil
- 1 teaspoon smoked paprika
- Salt and pepper to taste

How to Proceed:

1. Warm up oil in a skillet over medium-high heat.
2. Season the tofu slices with smoked paprika, salt, and pepper.
3. Fry the tofu slices for about 3-4 minutes on each side until crispy and golden.
4. Brush BBQ sauce on the tofu and cook for an additional 1-2 minutes on each side until caramelized.
5. Serve hot.

Nutritional Facts: Calories: 180 | Protein: 10g | Carbohydrates: 10g | Fat: 12g | Fiber: 1g

Green Detox Smoothie

What do you need (Serve 1):

- 1 cup fresh
- 1 small cucumber, chopped
- 1 apple, cored and sliced
- Juice of 1/2 lemon
- 1 tbsp chia seeds
- 1 cup water or coconut water

How to Proceed:

1. Combine every item in a food processor.
2. Process until smooth and creamy.
3. Serve chilled.

Nutritional Facts:
Calories: 140 | Protein: 3g | Carbohydrates: 27g | Fat: 3g | Fiber: 6g

Berry Blast Smoothie

What do you need (Serve 1):

- 1 cup mixed berries (strawberries, blueberries, raspberries, frozen or fresh)
- 1 banana
- 1/2 cup Greek yogurt
- 1/2 cup almond milk
- 1 tbsp honey or maple syrup

How to Proceed:

1. Combine every item in a food processor.
2. Process until creamy.
3. Pour into a glass and enjoy.

Nutritional Facts: Calories: 210 | Protein: 8g | Carbohydrates: 44g | Fat: 3g | Fiber: 5g

Almond Flour Pancakes

What do you need (Serve 2):
- 1 cup almond flour
- 2 eggs
- 1/4 cup water or almond milk
- 1 tbsp maple syrup
- 1/2 tsp GF baking powder
- Pinch of salt
- Butter or oil for cooking

How to Proceed:
1. Combine almond flour in a mixing container with baking powder, and salt.
2. In another bowl, whisk eggs and water or almond milk and maple syrup.
3. Mix the wet and dry ingredients until smooth.
4. Warm a non-stick skillet over medium heat and brush with butter or oil.
5. Pour small circles of batter onto the skillet. Cook for 2-3 minutes on each side until golden brown.
6. Serve with extra maple syrup or fresh fruits.

Nutritional Facts: Calories: 320 | Protein: 12g | Carbohydrates: 14g | Fat: 23g | Fiber: 3g

MAIN DISHES

Lemon Garlic Salmon

What do you need (Serve 2):

- 2 salmon fillets (6 oz each)
- 2 tablespoons olive/vegetable oil
- Juice and zest of 1 lemon
- 2 garlic cloves, minced
- Salt and pepper to taste
- Fresh parsley, chopped (for garnish)

How to Proceed:

1. Warm up the oil in a skillet over medium-high heat.
2. Season salmon fillets with salt and pepper.
3. Place salmon in the skillet, skin-side up, and cook for about 3-4 minutes until golden.
4. Flip the salmon, add minced garlic, and lemon zest around the fillets.
5. Squeeze lemon juice over the salmon and cook for few minutes until the fish is cooked through.
6. Garnish with fresh parsley before serving.

Nutritional Facts:
Calories: 300 | Protein: 23g | Carbohydrates: 1g | Fat: 23g | Fiber: 0g

Grilled Chicken Caesar Salad

What do you need (Serve 2):

- 2 chicken breasts
- Salt and pepper to taste
- 4 cups chopped romaine lettuce
- 1/4 cup grated Parmesan cheese
- 1/2 cup GF Caesar dressing
- GF croutons

How to Proceed:

1. Warm up grill to medium-high heat. Season chicken breasts with salt and pepper.
2. Grill chicken for about 5-6 minutes on each side or until fully cooked with clear juices.
3. Let it rest for a few minutes, then slice.
4. In a bowl, toss romaine lettuce with Caesar dressing, Parmesan cheese, and croutons.
5. Top salad with grilled chicken slices.
6. Serve immediately.

Nutritional Facts:
Calories: 350 | Protein: 28g | Carbohydrates: 12g | Fat: 20g | Fiber: 3g

Greek Feta Stuffed Mini Peppers

What do you need:

- 8 mini bell peppers, halved and seeded
- 1/2 cup crumbled feta cheese
- 1/4 cup chopped Kalamata olives
- 1 tbsp chopped fresh oregano
- 1 tbsp olive oil
- Black pepper to taste

How to Proceed:

1. In a bowl, mix crumbled feta, chopped olives, fresh oregano, and olive oil.
2. Spoon the feta and olive mixture into the halved mini peppers.
3. Arrange on a serving platter and sprinkle with black pepper.
4. Serve immediately.

Nutritional Facts: Calories: 100 | Protein: 3g | Carbohydrates: 4g | Fat: 8g | Fiber: 1g

Honey Glazed Shrimp

What do you need (Serve 4):

- 1 lb shrimp, peeled and deveined
- 2 tablespoons honey
- 1 tablespoon GF soy sauce or tamari sauce
- 1 garlic clove, minced
- 1 tablespoon olive oil
- Fresh cilantro, chopped (for garnish)

How to Proceed:

1. In a bowl, combine honey, GF soy sauce, and minced garlic.
2. Warm up olive oil in a skillet over medium-high heat.
3. Add shrimp and sauté for about 2 minutes.
4. Pour the honey mixture over the shrimp and continue to cook for another 2-3 minutes until shrimp are pink and coated with the glaze.
5. Garnish with chopped cilantro before serving.

Nutritional Facts: Calories: 240 | Protein: 24g | Carbohydrates: 19g | Fat: 8g | Fiber: 0g

Quinoa Pilaf

What do you need (Serve 4):

- 1 cup quinoa (rinsed and drained)
- 2 cups hot GF vegetable broth
- 1/2 cup diced carrots
- 1/2 cup diced bell peppers
- 1/4 cup finely chopped onions
- 2 tablespoons olive/vegetable oil
- Salt and pepper to taste
- Fresh parsley for garnish

How to Proceed:

1. Warm up the oil in a medium saucepan over medium heat.
2. Mix the onions, carrots, and bell peppers, and sauté until the vegetables are soft, about 5 minutes.
3. Stir in the quinoa and vegetable broth, bring to a boil.
4. Reduce heat to low, cover, and simmer for about 15 minutes, or until the liquid is absorbed and the quinoa is tender.
5. Fluff the quinoa with a fork, season with salt and pepper, and garnish with fresh parsley before serving.

Nutritional Facts:
Calories: 220 | Protein: 6g | Carbohydrates: 35g | Fat: 7g | Fiber: 4g

BRAIN-BOOSTING SNACKS & BITES

Cucumber and Smoked Salmon Bites

What do you need:

- 1 cucumber, sliced into rounds
- 4 oz smoked salmon, cut into small pieces
- 1 tbsp dairy-free cream cheese
- 1 tsp capers (optional)
- Fresh dill for garnish

How to Proceed:

1. Spread a small amount of dairy-free cream cheese on each cucumber round.
2. Top with a piece of smoked salmon.
3. Garnish with capers and fresh dill if desired.
4. Serve immediately.

Nutritional Facts: Calories: 100 | Protein: 6g | Carbohydrates: 2g | Fat: 7g | Fiber: 0g

Veggie Sushi Rolls

What do you need:

- 4 sheets nori (seaweed)
- 1 cup cooked sushi rice (cooled)
- 1/2 avocado, sliced
- 1/2 cucumber, julienned
- 1/2 carrot, julienned
- 1 tbsp GF soy sauce or tamari for dipping
- Optional: pickled ginger and wasabi

How to Proceed:

1. Lay a nori sheet shiny side down on a bamboo sushi mat.
2. Spread a thin layer of sushi rice over the nori, leaving a 1-inch border at the top.
3. Arrange avocado, cucumber, and carrot along the bottom edge of the rice.
4. Roll the nori tightly around the fillings, using the bamboo mat to shape the roll.
5. Slice into bite-sized pieces and serve with soy sauce, pickled ginger, and wasabi.

Nutritional Facts: Calories: 160 | Protein: 4g | Carbohydrates: 32g | Fat: 4g | Fiber: 3g

Garlic Parmesan Popcorn

What do you need (Serves 4):

- 1/2 cup popcorn kernels
- 3 tbsp olive/vegetable oil
- 1/4 cup grated Parmesan cheese (use nutritional yeast for a dairy-free version)
- 1 tsp garlic powder
- Salt to taste

How to Proceed:

1. Warm up the oil in a large pot over medium-high heat.
2. Add popcorn kernels and cover. Once popping begins, shake the pot occasionally until popping slows down.
3. Remove from heat and sprinkle garlic powder, Parmesan cheese, and salt over the popcorn. Cover and shake well to distribute the flavors.
4. Serve immediately.

Nutritional Facts:
Calories: 150 | Protein: 4g | Carbohydrates: 15g | Fat: 9g | Fiber: 3g

Avocado Salsa

What do you need (Serves 4):
- 2 ripe avocados, diced
- 1/2 cup diced tomatoes
- 1/4 cup finely chopped red onion
- 1 jalapeño, seeded and finely chopped
- Juice of 1 lime
- 1/4 cup chopped cilantro
- Salt and pepper to taste

How to Proceed:
1. In a medium bowl, combine diced avocados, tomatoes, red onion, jalapeño, and cilantro.
2. Squeeze lime juice over the mixture and gently stir to combine.
3. Season with salt and pepper to taste.
4. Serve immediately with GF tortilla chips, or cover and refrigerate until serving.

Nutritional Facts:
Calories: 140 | Protein: 2g | Carbohydrates: 10g | Fat: 12g | Fiber: 4g

Mini Bell Pepper Nachos

What do you need (Serves 4):
- 12 mini bell peppers, halved and seeded
- 1 cup cooked and shredded chicken
- 1/2 cup black beans, rinsed and drained
- 1/2 cup shredded cheese (dairy-free if needed)
- 1/4 cup sliced black olives
- 1/4 cup salsa
- 1/4 cup guacamole

How to Proceed:
1. Warm up your oven to 375°F (190°C).
2. Arrange bell pepper halves on a baking sheet.
3. Spoon a small amount of chicken, black beans, and black olives into each bell pepper half.
4. Top each with a sprinkle of shredded cheese.
5. Bake in the preheated oven for about 10 minutes or until the cheese is melted and peppers are slightly tender.
6. Serve with salsa and guacamole on the side.

Nutritional Facts: Calories: 150 | Protein: 10g | Carbohydrates: 8g | Fat: 9g | Fiber: 3g

Spicy Tuna Stuffed Cucumber Cups

What do you need:
- 2 large cucumbers, cut into 1-inch thick slices
- 1 can (5 oz) tuna, drained and flaked
- 1/4 cup mayonnaise (dairy-free if needed)
- 1 tsp sriracha or other hot sauce
- 1 tbsp chopped fresh chives
- Salt and pepper to taste

How to Proceed:
1. Using a melon baller or small spoon, scoop out the center of each cucumber slice to create a cup.
2. In a small bowl, mix tuna, mayonnaise, sriracha, and chives. Season with salt and pepper.
3. Spoon the tuna mixture into the cucumber cups.
4. Chill in the refrigerator for about 10 minutes before serving.

Nutritional Facts: Calories: 70 (per stuffed cucumber) | Protein: 5g | Carbohydrates: 2g | Fat: 5g | Fiber: 0.5g

CHAPTER 4. BALANCED DAILY DISHES

These gluten-free side dishes and snacks are designed for efficiency and simplicity; each recipe provides delightful flavors and essential nutrients, perfect for complementing any meal or for a quick snack during the day.

COOKING TIME-SAVING TIPS

#1: The following sides can be cooked in larger quantities and stored in the fridge for 2-3 days and paired with various dishes in the following days to reduce cooking time.

#2: Heating water or broth in a kettle significantly reduces cooking time.

SOUP & STEW

Sweet Corn Chowder

What do you need (Serve 4):

- 2 cups frozen sweet corn
- 1 cup diced potatoes
- 1/2 cup diced onion
- 2 cups hot GF vegetable broth
- 1 cup cream or full-fat coconut milk for a dairy-free option
- Salt and pepper to taste
- Olive oil for sautéing

How to Proceed:
1. In a pot, warm up a splash of oil over medium heat.
2. Combine the onions and potatoes, sautéing until the onions are translucent.
3. Mix the sweet corn and vegetable broth, bringing the mixture to a boil.
4. Bring down to a quiet simmer until the potatoes are tender, about 10 minutes.
5. Stir in the cream or coconut milk, heating through.
6. Season with salt and pepper to taste.
7. Serve hot, optionally garnished with fresh herbs or green onions.

Nutritional Facts: Calories: 220 | Protein: 4g | Carbohydrates: 27g | Fat: 12g | Fiber: 3g

Butternut Squash Soup

What do you need (Serve 4):

- 2 cups cubed butternut squash
- 1 apple, peeled and chopped
- 1/2 cup chopped onion
- 3 cups hot GF vegetable broth
- 1/2 tsp ground cinnamon
- 1/4 tsp nutmeg
- Salt and pepper to taste
- Olive oil for sautéing

How to Proceed:
1. In a pot, warm up oil over medium heat.
2. Incorporate the onion and apple, sauté until the onion is translucent.
3. Combine the butternut squash, vegetable broth, cinnamon, and nutmeg.
4. Bring to a boil, then reduce heat and simmer until the squash is soft, about 15 minutes.
5. Use a food processor to purée the soup until smooth. Season with salt and pepper to taste.
6. Serve hot, garnished with a dollop of yogurt or a sprinkle of toasted pumpkin seeds.

Nutritional Facts: Calories: 150 | Protein: 2g | Carbohydrates: 35g | Fat: 1g | Fiber: 6g

Chicken and Vegetable Soup

What do you need (Serve 4):

- 1 cup cooked, shredded chicken
- 2 cups mixed vegetables (carrots, peas, and corn)
- 4 cups hot GF chicken broth
- 1 tsp dried thyme
- Salt and pepper to taste

How to Proceed:

1. In a large pot, bring the chicken broth to a boil.
2. Incorporate the mixed vegetables, thyme, and cooked chicken.
3. Bring down to a quiet simmer and cook for about 10 minutes until vegetables are tender.
4. Season with salt and pepper to taste.
5. Serve hot.

Nutritional Facts:
Calories: 180 | Protein: 18g | Carbohydrates: 13g | Fat: 5g | Fiber: 3g

Lentil Soup

What do you need (Serve 4):

- 1 cup dried lentils, rinsed
- 4 cups hot GF vegetable broth
- 1/2 cup chopped onion
- 2 garlic cloves, minced
- 1 tsp ground cumin
- Salt and pepper to taste
- Olive oil for sautéing or any kind of oil

How to Proceed:

1. In a pot, warm up vegetable oil over medium heat.
2. Mix onion with garlic, and sauté until onion is translucent, about 3 minutes.
3. Incorporate lentils, vegetable broth, and cumin.
4. Heat until bubbling, then lower temperature and cook gently until lentils soften, about 15 minutes.
5. Season with salt and pepper to taste.
6. Serve hot, garnished with fresh herbs if desired.

Nutritional Facts:
Calories: 230 | Protein: 15g | Carbohydrates: 33g |Fat: 4g | Fiber: 15g

VEGETARIAN AND VEGAN MAIN DISHES

Creating quick, delicious, and satisfying vegetarian and vegan main dishes that are also gluten-free can be simple with the right recipes. Each of these dishes is designed to be prepared in 15 minutes or less, perfect for a busy lifestyle.

Cauliflower Steaks

What do you need (Serve 4):

- 1 large head cauliflower
- 2 tablespoons olive oil
- 1 teaspoon garlic powder
- 1 teaspoon smoked paprika
- Salt and pepper to taste

How to Proceed:

1. Slice the cauliflower into 1/2 inch thick steaks from the center of the cauliflower to ensure they hold together.
2. Brush each steak with olive oil and sprinkle with garlic powder, smoked paprika, salt, and pepper.
3. Heat a grill pan or skillet over medium heat and grill the cauliflower steaks for about 5-7 minutes on each side, until charred and tender.
4. Serve hot with a drizzle of tahini or your favorite vegan sauce.

Nutritional Facts: Calories: 120 | Protein: 4g | Carbohydrates: 10g | Fat: 7g | Fiber: 5g

Lentil Shepherd's Pie

What do you need (Serve 4):

- 2 cups cooked lentils
- 1 cup frozen mixed vegetables (carrots, peas, and corn)
- 1/2 cup GF vegetable broth
- 1 teaspoon dried thyme
- Salt and pepper to taste
- 2 cups mashed potatoes (prepared ahead or instant GF mashed potatoes)

How to Proceed:

1. Warm up your oven to 400°F (200°C) if you choose to bake.
2. In a skillet, combine lentils, frozen vegetables, vegetable broth, thyme, salt, and pepper. Cook over medium heat for about 5-7 minutes until the vegetables are heated through.
3. Move the lentil mixture into a baking dish if baking, or keep in the skillet if serving directly.
4. Top with a layer of mashed potatoes.
5. If baking, place in the oven and bake for about 10 minutes until slightly golden.
6. Serve hot.

Nutritional Facts: Calories: 280 | Protein: 14g | Carbohydrates: 42g | Fat: 4g | Fiber: 10g

Mushroom Stir-Fry

What do you need (Serve 3):

- 2 cups sliced mushrooms
- 1 bell pepper, sliced
- 1 onion, sliced
- 2 tablespoons GF soy sauce or tamari sauce
- 1 tablespoon sesame oil
- 1 teaspoon grated ginger
- 1 garlic clove, minced

How to Proceed:
1. Warm up sesame oil in a skillet or wok over medium-high heat.
2. Mix in garlic and ginger, and sauté for few minutes until fragrant.
3. Combine mushrooms, bell pepper, and onion. Stir-fry for about 5-7 minutes until vegetables are tender and slightly browned.
4. Drizzle GF soy sauce over the vegetables and stir to combine.
5. Serve; use sesame seeds to garnish.

Nutritional Facts: Calories: 120 | Protein: 4g | Carbohydrates: 10g | Fat: 8g | Fiber: 2g

Vegan Chili

What do you need (Serve 4):

- 1 can (15 oz) black beans, rinsed and drained
- 1 can (15 oz) kidney beans, rinsed and drained
- 1 can (15 oz) diced tomatoes with juice
- 1 onion, chopped
- 2 cloves garlic, minced
- 2 tablespoons chili powder
- 1 teaspoon cumin
- 1/2 teaspoon paprika
- 1/2 cup hot GF vegetable broth
- Salt and pepper to taste
- Olive oil for sautéing

How to Proceed:
1. Warm up a large pot over medium heat and add some oil.
2. Sauté the onion and garlic until translucent.
3. Add chili powder, cumin, and paprika, cooking for about 1 minute until fragrant.
4. Stir in the black beans, kidney beans, diced tomatoes, and vegetable broth.
5. Heat until boiling, then lower the heat and let it simmer for about 10 minutes to blend the flavors.
6. Add salt and pepper to taste.
7. Serve hot, topped with vegan sour cream or chopped green onions if desired.

Nutritional Facts: Calories: 210 | Protein: 12g | Carbohydrates: 35g | Fat: 3g | Fiber: 10g

Vegan Alfredo Pasta

What do you need (Serve 4):

- 8 oz GF fettuccine
- 1 cup cauliflower florets
- 1/2 cup raw cashews, soaked for at least 2 hours (or almond butter)
- 1/2 cup unsweetened almond milk or substitute
- 2 cloves garlic, minced
- 2 tablespoons nutritional yeast
- 1 tablespoon lemon juice
- Salt and pepper to taste
- Chopped parsley for garnish

How to Proceed:
1. Prepare the g fettuccine as directed on the package, then drain and set it aside.
2. In a saucepan, boil cauliflower florets until tender, about 7 minutes.
3. In a food processor, combine cooked cauliflower, soaked cashews, almond milk, garlic, nutritional yeast, and lemon juice. Blend until smooth and creamy.
4. Toss the pasta with the cauliflower Alfredo sauce and heat through if necessary.
5. Season with salt and pepper, and garnish with chopped parsley before serving.

Nutritional Facts: Calories: 320 | Protein: 12g | Carbohydrates: 49g | Fat: 9g | Fiber: 6g

FISH AND POULTRY MAIN DISHES

Here are some delicious, quick-prep fish and poultry recipes that you can easily incorporate into your busy schedule. Each dish is packed with flavor and can be prepared easily.

Baked Cod with Herbs

What do you need (Serve 2):

- 2 cod fillets (6 oz each)
- 1 tablespoon olive/vegetable oil
- 1 teaspoon dried Italian herbs
- Salt and pepper to taste
- Lemon slices (for serving)

How to Proceed:

1. Warm up your oven to 400°F (200°C).
2. Place the cod fillets in a baking dish and brush with oil.
3. Sprinkle dried herbs, salt, and pepper evenly over the cod.
4. Bake in the oven for about 10-12 minutes, until the fish is flaky and opaque.
5. Serve with lemon slices on the side.

Nutritional Facts:
Calories: 190 | Protein: 20g | Carbohydrates: 0g | Fat: 12g | Fiber: 0g

Grilled Tilapia Tacos

What do you need (Serve 2):

- 2 tilapia fillets
- 1 tablespoon olive/vegetable oil
- 1 teaspoon chili powder
- 1/2 teaspoon cumin
- Salt and pepper to taste
- GF corn tortillas
- Fresh salsa, shredded lettuce, and lime wedges for serving

How to Proceed:

1. Preheat grill or grill pan to medium-high heat.
2. Brush tilapia fillets with olive oil and season with chili powder, cumin, salt, and pepper.
3. Grill tilapia for about 3-4 minutes on each side, until fully cooked and easily flaked with a fork.
4. Break the tilapia into pieces and serve on warm GF corn tortillas with salsa, lettuce, and a squeeze of lime.

Nutritional Facts:
Calories: 210 | Protein: 23g | Carbohydrates: 9g | Fat: 10g | Fiber: 2g

Chicken Stir-Fry

What do you need (Serve 2):

- 2 chicken breasts, thinly sliced
- 1 bell pepper, julienned
- 1 cup broccoli florets
- 2 tablespoons olive/vegetable oil
- 2 tablespoons GF soy sauce
- 1 tablespoon honey
- 1 garlic clove, minced
- 1 teaspoon grated ginger
- Salt and pepper to taste
- Sesame seeds for garnish

How to Proceed:

1. Warm up olive oil in a large skillet over medium-high heat.
2. Incorporate chicken slices and stir-fry until they start to brown, about 3-4 minutes.
3. Incorporate the bell pepper and broccoli, cooking until they are just tender, about 3-4 more minutes.
4. Mix GF soy sauce, honey, minced garlic, and grated ginger in a small bowl.
5. Pour the sauce over the chicken and vegetables in the skillet, stirring to coat evenly.
6. Cook for another 2 minutes until everything is heated through and well coated.
7. Season with salt and pepper.

Nutritional Facts:
Calories: 300 | Protein: 26g | Carbohydrates: 12g | Fat: 16g | Fiber: 2g

Tuna Salad Lettuce Wraps

What do you need (Serve 2):

- 1 can (5 oz) tuna, drained
- 1/4 cup GF mayonnaise
- 1/4 cup diced celery
- 1 tablespoon lemon juice
- Salt and pepper to taste
- Lettuce leaves (such as Bibb or iceberg) for wrapping

How to Proceed:

1. In a bowl, mix tuna, mayonnaise, diced celery, lemon juice, salt, and pepper.
2. Spoon the tuna mixture into lettuce leaves.
3. Serve immediately as wraps.

Nutritional Facts:
Calories: 180 | Protein: 12g | Carbohydrates: 1g | Fat: 14g | Fiber: 0g

Thai Coconut Chicken

What do you need (Serve 2):

- 2 chicken breasts, cut into bite-sized pieces
- 1 can (14 oz) coconut milk
- 1 tablespoon Thai red curry paste
- 1 tablespoon GF fish sauce
- 1 tablespoon brown sugar
- 1/2 cup diced bell peppers
- 1/2 cup snap peas
- Fresh basil leaves for garnish
- 1 tablespoon olive/vegetable oil

How to Proceed:

1. Heat oil in a skillet over medium-high heat.
2. Add chicken pieces and cook until they start to brown, about 3-4 minutes.
3. Stir in Thai red curry paste, cooking for another minute until fragrant.
4. Pour in coconut milk, fish sauce, and brown sugar. Bring to a simmer.
5. Add bell peppers and snap peas, and simmer for about 5 minutes until the vegetables are tender and the chicken is cooked through.
6. Garnish with basil leaves.

Nutritional Facts:
Calories: 420 | Protein: 25g | Carbohydrates: 12g | Fat: 32g | Fiber: 2g

Baked Herb Chicken Breasts

What do you need (Serve 2):

- 2 chicken breasts
- 2 tablespoons olive/vegetable oil
- 1 teaspoon dried basil
- 1 teaspoon dried oregano
- 1/2 teaspoon garlic powder
- Salt and pepper to taste
- Lemon wedges for serving

How to Proceed:

1. Warm up your oven to 400°F (200°C).
2. Rub each chicken breast with olive oil and sprinkle with basil, oregano, garlic powder, salt, and pepper.
3. Place the chicken in a baking dish and bake for about 12-15 minutes, until the chicken is fully cooked and the juices run clear.
4. Serve with lemon wedges on the side.

Nutritional Facts:
Calories: 265 | Protein: 25g | Carbohydrates: 1g | Fat: 18g | Fiber: 1g

Turkey Meatballs

What do you need (Serve 2):

- 1 pound ground turkey
- 1/4 cup GF breadcrumbs
- 1 egg
- 2 cloves garlic, minced
- 1 teaspoon Italian seasoning
- Salt and pepper to taste
- 1 tablespoon olive/vegetable oil

How to Proceed:

1. In a bowl, combine ground turkey, GF breadcrumbs, egg, minced garlic, Italian seasoning, salt, and pepper.
2. Combine well and form into small balls.
3. Warm up olive oil in a skillet over medium heat.
4. Add meatballs and cook, turning occasionally, until browned and cooked through, about 10-12 minutes.
5. Serve hot with your favorite GF pasta and sauce or enjoy as a standalone dish with a side of veggies.

Nutritional Facts:
Calories: 220 | Protein: 20g | Carbohydrates: 5g | Fat: 13g | Fiber: 1g

Chicken Fajitas

What do you need (Serve 2):

- 2 chicken breasts, thinly sliced
- 1 bell pepper, sliced
- 1 onion, sliced
- 2 tablespoons olive oil
- 1 tablespoon lime juice
- 1 teaspoon chili powder
- 1 teaspoon cumin
- Salt and pepper to taste
- GF tortillas for serving

How to Proceed:

1. Warm up olive oil in a large skillet over medium-high heat.
2. Incorporate the chicken slices and cook until no longer pink, about 3-4 minutes.
3. Incorporate bell pepper and onion, and continue to cook until the vegetables are soft, about 3-4 more minutes.
4. Season with chili powder, cumin, salt, and pepper.
5. Drizzle lime juice over the chicken and vegetables just before removing from heat.
6. Serve hot with tortillas.

Nutritional Facts:
Calories: 280 | Protein: 26g | Carbohydrates: 9g | Fat: 16g | Fiber: 2g

Quick Shrimp Stir-Fry

What do you need (Serve 2):

- 1 lb shrimp, peeled and deveined
- 2 cups mixed vegetables (like bell peppers, snap peas, and carrots), thinly sliced
- 2 tablespoons GF soy sauce
- 1 tablespoon sesame oil
- 1 teaspoon minced ginger
- 1 garlic clove, minced
- Salt and pepper to taste

How to Proceed:

1. Warm up sesame oil in a large skillet or wok over medium-high heat.
2. Incorporate minced garlic and ginger; sauté for 30 seconds until fragrant.
3. Incorporate shrimp and stir-fry for about 2-3 minutes until pink and almost fully cooked.
4. Add mixed vegetables and GF soy sauce. Stir-fry for an additional 3-4 minutes until vegetables are just tender and shrimp are cooked through.
5. Season with salt and pepper to taste.
6. Serve, garnished with sesame seeds.

Nutritional Facts:
Calories: 240 | Protein: 24g | Carbohydrates: 8g | Fat: 13g | Fiber: 1g

Lemon Herb Baked Tilapia

What do you need (Serve 4):

- 4 tilapia fillets
- 2 tablespoons olive/vegetable oil
- Juice and zest of 1 lemon
- 1 teaspoon dried herbs (such as thyme, oregano, or dill)
- Salt and pepper to taste

How to Proceed:

1. Warm up oven to 400°F (200°C).
2. Place tilapia fillets in a baking dish. Drizzle with olive oil and lemon juice. Sprinkle with lemon zest, dried herbs, salt, and pepper.
3. Bake in the preheated oven for about 10-12 minutes, or until fish flakes easily with a fork.
4. Serve hot, garnished with additional herbs or lemon slices if desired.

Nutritional Facts:
Calories: 180 | Protein: 23g | Carbohydrates: 1g | Fat: 10g | Fiber: 0g

BEEF AND PORK MAIN DISHES

For those evenings when you're craving a hearty meal but are short on time, these quick beef and pork dishes fit the bill perfectly, and delivers on both taste and nutrition.

Beef and Broccoli Stir-Fry

What do you need:

- 1 lb beef sirloin, thinly sliced
- 2 cups broccoli florets
- 2 tablespoons olive oil
- 2 cloves garlic, minced
- 1/4 cup GF soy sauce
- 1 tablespoon cornstarch
- 1/2 cup water
- 1 tablespoon sesame oil or any oil
- Salt and pepper to taste

How to Proceed:

5. Warm up olive oil in a large skillet over medium-high heat.
6. Combine garlic and beef slices, stir-fry for about 3-4 minutes until the beef is nearly cooked through.
7. Mix GF soy sauce, cornstarch, and water in a bowl until smooth.
8. Add broccoli to the skillet, pour the soy sauce mixture over the beef and broccoli. Cook for another 3-4 minutes, stirring frequently, until the sauce thickens and broccoli is tender but crisp.
9. Drizzle with oil, season with salt and pepper, and serve hot.

Nutritional Facts:
Calories: 320 | Protein: 23g | Carbohydrates: 10g | Fat: 20g | Fiber: 2g

Gluten-Free Meatloaf

What do you need:

- 1 lb ground beef
- 1 egg
- 1/2 cup GF breadcrumbs
- 1/4 cup ketchup
- 1 onion, finely chopped
- 1 teaspoon GF Worcestershire sauce
- Salt and pepper to taste

How to Proceed:

1. Warm up your oven to 375°F (190°C) if using an oven or prepare a microwave-safe dish if using a microwave.
2. In a bowl, mix ground beef, egg, breadcrumbs, ketchup, onion, Worcestershire sauce, salt, and pepper.
3. Press the mixture into a loaf shape on a baking tray or a microwave-safe dish.
4. Bake in the preheated oven for about 45 minutes or microwave on high for 6-8 minutes until the meat is cooked through.
5. Let rest before slicing. Serve hot.

Nutritional Facts:
Calories: 360 | Protein: 25g | Carbohydrates: 15g | Fat: 20g | Fiber: 2g

Spaghetti Bolognese

What do you need:

- 1 lb ground beef
- 2 cups GF spaghetti
- 1 can (15 oz) tomato sauce
- 1 onion, chopped
- 2 cloves garlic, minced
- 1 tablespoon olive oil
- 1 teaspoon dried basil
- Salt and pepper to taste
- Grated Parmesan cheese (optional)

How to Proceed:

1. Cook GF spaghetti according to package instructions. Drain and set aside.
2. In the meantime warm up oil in a skillet over medium heat. Add onion and garlic, sauté until translucent.
3. Combine ground beef, breaking it apart with a spatula, and cook until browned.
4. Stir in tomato sauce and basil. Season with salt and pepper. Simmer for about 8-10 minutes, stirring occasionally.
5. Serve the sauce over the cooked spaghetti. Top with grated Parmesan cheese if desired.

Nutritional Facts:
Calories: 560 | Protein: 35g | Carbohydrates: 60g | Fat: 20g | Fiber: 4g

Beef Tacos

What do you need:

- 1 lb ground beef
- 1 tablespoon olive/vegetable oil
- 1 packet GF taco seasoning
- 1/2 cup water
- GF corn tortillas

Toppings: shredded lettuce, diced tomatoes, sliced jalapeños, shredded cheese (optional), and salsa

How to Proceed:

1. Warm up oil in a skillet over medium heat. Mix the ground beef and cook until browned, breaking it up with a spoon, about 5-7 minutes.
2. Drain excess fat and return skillet to heat. Stir in the GF taco seasoning and water.
3. Bring to a simmer and cook until thickened, about 5 minutes.
4. Warm the GF corn tortillas in a dry skillet or microwave.
5. Assemble the tacos by spooning the beef mixture into tortillas and topping with lettuce, tomatoes, jalapeños, cheese, and salsa.
6. Serve immediately.

Nutritional Facts:
Calories: 320 | Protein: 25g | Carbohydrates: 20g | Fat: 15g | Fiber: 3g

Pork Stir-Fry

What do you need:

- 1 lb pork tenderloin, thinly sliced
- 2 cups mixed vegetables (broccoli, bell peppers, carrots)
- 2 tablespoons GF soy sauce
- 1 tablespoon honey
- 1 tablespoon sesame oil
- 1 garlic clove, minced
- 1 teaspoon grated ginger
- Salt and pepper to taste

How to Proceed:

1. Warm up sesame oil in a large skillet or wok over medium-high heat.
2. Mix pork slices and stir-fry until they start to brown, about 3-4 minutes.
3. Add garlic, ginger, and vegetables, and continue to stir-fry until vegetables are just tender, about 3-4 minutes.
4. Mix GF soy sauce and honey, pour over the stir-fry, and mix well.
5. Season with salt and pepper to taste.
6. Serve hot, garnished with sesame seeds.

Nutritional Facts:
Calories: 280 | Protein: 26g | Carbohydrates: 16g | Fat: 12g | Fiber: 3g

Grilled Pork Chops

What do you need:

- 4 pork chops, about 1 inch thick
- 2 tablespoons olive/vegetable oil
- 1 teaspoon garlic powder
- 1 teaspoon smoked paprika
- Salt and pepper to taste

How to Proceed:

1. Warm up your grill to medium-high heat.
2. Rub each pork chop with olive oil and then season with garlic powder, smoked paprika, salt, and pepper.
3. Grill the pork chops for about 5-7 minutes on each side, depending on thickness, until the internal temperature reaches 145°F (63°C) and they are nicely charred.
4. Let rest for 3 minutes before serving to allow juices to redistribute.

Nutritional Facts:
Calories: 290 | Protein: 38g | Carbohydrates: 0g | Fat: 15g | Fiber: 0g

Sausage and Peppers

What do you need:

- 1 lb pork sausages
- 2 bell peppers, sliced
- 1 onion, sliced
- 2 tablespoons olive/vegetable oil
- Salt and pepper to taste

How to Proceed:

1. Warm up oil in a large skillet over medium heat.
2. Add the sausages and cook until browned on all sides, about 5-7 minutes.
3. Remove the sausages and set aside. In the same skillet, add the sliced bell peppers and onion. Season with salt and pepper.
4. Sauté until the vegetables are soft and caramelized, about 5 minutes.
5. Slice the sausages and return them to the skillet with the vegetables. Cook for an additional 2-3 minutes to heat through.
6. Serve hot.

Nutritional Facts:
Calories: 450 | Protein: 23g | Carbohydrates: 8g | Fat: 36g | Fiber: 2g

Quick Beef Stir-Fry

What do you need:

- 1 lb thinly sliced beef strips (such as sirloin or flank steak)
- 2 cups of mixed stir-fry vegetables (cabbage, carrots, bell peppers)
- 2 tablespoons GF soy sauce
- 1 tablespoon GF hoisin sauce
- 1 teaspoon sesame/vegetable oil
- 2 cloves garlic, minced
- 1 teaspoon grated ginger
- 1 tablespoon vegetable oil

How to Proceed:

1. Warm up vegetable oil in a large skillet or wok over high heat.
2. Add beef strips and stir-fry until they start to brown, about 2-3 minutes.
3. Mix garlic and ginger, and stir-fry for another minute until fragrant.
4. Add the vegetables, GF soy sauce, hoisin sauce, and sesame oil. Continue to stir-fry until the vegetables are tender-crisp, about 3-4 minutes.
5. Serve immediately.

Nutritional Facts: Calories: 250 | Protein: 25g | Carbohydrates: 10g | Fat: 12g | Fiber: 2g

Peppered Pork Tenderloin

What do you need:

- 1 pork tenderloin, about 1 lb
- 1 tablespoon black peppercorns, crushed
- 1 teaspoon salt
- 2 tablespoons olive/vegetable oil
- 1/4 cup balsamic vinegar

How to Proceed:

1. Rub the pork tenderloin with crushed peppercorns and salt.
2. Warm up oil in a large skillet over medium-high heat.
3. Add pork tenderloin and sear on all sides until golden brown, about 1-2 minutes per side.
4. Reduce heat to medium, add balsamic vinegar and cover.
5. Cook for about 6-8 minutes, turning occasionally, until the pork reaches an internal temperature of 145°F (63°C).
6. Remove from heat, let rest for a few minutes, then slice and serve drizzled with the pan juices.

Nutritional Facts: Calories: 280 | Protein: 30g | Carbohydrates: 3g | Fat: 16g | Fiber: 0g

EGGS AND DAIRY-FREE OPTIONS

Here are several gluten-free, egg-free, and dairy-free recipes that are simple to prepare and perfect for quick meals or snacks. These dishes ensure you don't compromise on taste or nutrition, even with dietary restrictions.

Tofu Scramble

What do you need:

- 1 block firm tofu, drained and crumbled
- 1 tbsp olive/vegetable oil
- 1/2 onion, diced
- 1/2 bell pepper, diced
- 1 tsp turmeric for color
- 1/2 tsp garlic powder
- Salt and pepper to taste
- 1 tbsp nutritional yeast (optional, for a cheesy flavor)
- Fresh herbs like parsley or cilantro, for garnish

How to Proceed:

1. Warm up oil in a skillet over medium heat.
2. Mix the onion and bell pepper, sautéing until soft, about 5 minutes.
3. Stir in the crumbled tofu, turmeric, garlic powder, salt, and pepper.
4. Cook for about 5-7 minutes, stirring occasionally until the tofu is heated through and slightly crispy.
5. Stir in nutritional yeast if using, to boost the flavor.
6. Garnish with fresh herbs before serving.

Nutritional Facts: Calories: 150 | Protein: 10g | Carbohydrates: 5g | Fat: 10g | Fiber: 2g

Vegan Banana Pancakes

What do you need:

- 1 cup oat flour
- 1 ripe banana, mashed
- 1 cup almond milk
- 1 tsp baking powder
- 1 tbsp maple syrup
- 1/2 tsp vanilla extract
- Pinch of salt
- Cooking spray or vegetable oil

How to Proceed:

1. In a mixing bowl, combine oat flour, baking powder, and salt.
2. Add the mashed banana, almond milk, maple syrup, and vanilla extract to the dry ingredients. Mix to combine well.
3. Warm up a non-stick skillet over medium heat and lightly grease with cooking spray or oil.
4. Pour about 1/4 cup of batter for each pancake onto the hot skillet. Cook for about 2-3 minutes on each side or until golden brown and cooked through.
5. Serve warm with additional maple syrup or fresh fruit.

Nutritional Facts: Calories: 180 | Protein: 4g | Carbohydrates: 32g | Fat: 4g | Fiber: 2g

Chickpea Omelette

What do you need:

- 1/2 cup chickpea flour (gram flour)
- 1/2 cup water
- 1/2 tsp turmeric
- 1/2 tsp baking powder
- Salt and pepper to taste
- 1/4 cup diced tomatoes
- 1/4 cup chopped spinach
- 1 tbsp olive/vegetable oil

How to Proceed:

1. In a pot, mix chickpea flour, water, turmeric, baking powder, salt, and pepper until smooth.
2. Stir in diced tomatoes and chopped spinach.
3. Warm up oil in a non-stick skillet over medium heat.
4. Pour the batter into the skillet, spreading it out to cover the surface. Cook for about 4-5 minutes, or until the edges start to lift from the pan.
5. Carefully flip the omelette and cook for another 3-4 minutes on the other side.
6. Serve hot.

Nutritional Facts: Calories: 200 | Protein: 8g | Carbohydrates: 20g | Fat: 10g | Fiber: 5g

Dairy-Free Mac and Cheese

What do you need:

- 2 cups GF pasta
- 1 cup raw cashews, soaked for 4 hours then drained
- 1 cup water
- 1/4 cup nutritional yeast
- 1 tsp garlic powder
- 1 tsp onion powder
- 1/2 tsp turmeric
- Salt and pepper to taste
- 1 tbsp lemon juice

How to Proceed:

1. Cook the GF pasta according to package instructions. Drain and set aside.
2. In the meanwhile in a food processor, combine soaked cashews, water, nutritional yeast, garlic powder, onion powder, turmeric, lemon juice, salt, and pepper. Blend until smooth and creamy.
3. Pour the cashew sauce over the cooked pasta in a pot. Heat over medium heat, stirring until the pasta is evenly coated and the sauce is heated through.
4. Serve immediately, seasoned with additional pepper or paprika if desired.

Nutritional Facts:
Calories: 350 | Protein: 12g | Carbohydrates: 48g | Fat: 14g | Fiber: 5g

Coconut Curry Chicken

What do you need:
- 1 lb chicken breast, cut into bite-sized pieces
- 1 tablespoon coconut/vegetable oil
- 1 onion, finely chopped
- 1 bell pepper, chopped
- 2 cloves garlic, minced
- 1 tablespoon curry powder
- 1 can (14 oz) coconut milk
- Salt and pepper to taste
- Fresh cilantro for garnish

How to Proceed:

1. Warm up coconut oil in a large skillet over medium heat.
2. Incorporate onion, bell pepper, and garlic, and sauté until the onion is translucent, about 5 minutes.
3. Stir in curry powder and cook for an additional minute until fragrant.
4. Add chicken pieces, seasoning with salt and pepper, and sauté until the chicken is mostly cooked through, about 5-7 minutes.
5. Pour in coconut milk and bring to a simmer. Let cook for another 5 minutes, or until the chicken is done and the sauce has thickened slightly.
6. Garnish with fresh cilantro before serving.

Nutritional Facts:
Calories: 330 | Protein: 25g | Carbohydrates: 8g | Fat: 24g | Fiber: 2g

Egg-Free Banana Pancakes

What do you need:
- 1 cup GF polenta
- 4 cups hot water or vegetable broth
- 1/2 teaspoon salt
- 2 tablespoons olive/vegetable oil
- 1 onion, chopped
- 2 cups sliced mushrooms
- 2 cups fresh spinach
- Salt and pepper to taste

How to Proceed:

1. In a saucepan, bring water or vegetable broth to a boil. Gradually whisk in polenta and salt, reduce heat to low, and cook, stirring often, until polenta is thick and creamy, about 10-15 minutes.
2. In another skillet, warm up oil over medium heat. Add onion and mushrooms and cook until softened, about 5-7 minutes.
3. Mix spinach and cook until just wilted, about 2-3 minutes. Season as desired.
4. Serve the mushroom and spinach mixture over the warm polenta.

Nutritional Facts:
Calories: 250 | Protein: 6g | Carbohydrates: 38g | Fat: 9g | Fiber: 4g

Tomato Basil Bruschetta

What do you need:

- 4 slices GF baguette or bread
- 1 cup diced tomatoes
- 2 tbsp chopped fresh basil
- 1 clove garlic, minced
- 1 tbsp olive oil
- 1 tsp balsamic vinegar
- Salt and pepper to taste

How to Proceed:

1. Toast the gluten-free bread slices until crispy.
2. In a bowl, combine diced tomatoes, basil, garlic, olive oil, balsamic vinegar, salt, and pepper.
3. Spoon the tomato mixture onto each slice of toasted bread.
4. Serve immediately as a quick and fresh appetizer.

Nutritional Facts: Calories: 150 | Protein: 3g | Carbohydrates: 20g | Fat: 6g | Fiber: 2g

Egg-Free Quinoa and Veggie Stir-Fry

What do you need:

- 1 cup cooked quinoa
- 1/2 cup chopped bell peppers
- 1/2 cup chopped broccoli
- 1/4 cup sliced carrots
- 2 tbsp tamari (GF soy sauce)
- 1 tbsp olive oil
- 1 clove garlic, minced
- 1/2 tsp ginger, minced

How to Proceed:

1. Heat olive oil in a large skillet over medium-high heat.
2. Add garlic and ginger, sauté for 1 minute.
3. Add bell peppers, broccoli, and carrots; stir-fry for 3-4 minutes until tender.
4. Stir in cooked quinoa and tamari, cooking for another 2 minutes.
5. Serve immediately.

Nutritional Facts: Calories: 230 | Protein: 7g | Carbohydrates: 35g | Fat: 7g | Fiber: 5g

Egg-Free Veggie Wrap

What do you need:

- 1 GF tortilla or wrap
- 1/4 cup hummus
- 1/4 cup shredded carrots
- 1/4 cup sliced cucumbers
- 1/4 cup spinach leaves
- 2 tbsp sliced avocado
- Salt and pepper to taste

How to Proceed:

1. Spread hummus evenly over the GF tortilla.
2. Layer with shredded carrots, cucumbers, spinach, and avocado slices.
3. Season with salt and pepper to taste.
4. Roll the wrap tightly, slice in half if desired.
5. Serve immediately.

Nutritional Facts: Calories: 220 | Protein: 5g | Carbohydrates: 30g | Fat: 10g | Fiber: 6g

GLOBAL FLAVORS

Delve into the world of international cuisine with these quick, gluten-free recipes that bring global flavors right to your kitchen. Each dish can be prepared in 15 minutes or less, offering a delicious and hassle-free way to enjoy diverse tastes.

Mexican Quinoa Salad

What do you need:

- 1 cup cooked quinoa
- 1/2 cup canned black beans, rinsed and drained
- 1/2 cup corn kernels
- 1/2 cup diced tomatoes
- 1/4 cup chopped fresh cilantro
- 1 avocado, diced
- Juice of 1 lime
- 2 tablespoons olive/vegetable oil
- 1 teaspoon cumin
- Salt and pepper to taste

How to Proceed:

1. In a bowl, incorporate quinoa, black beans, corn, tomatoes, cilantro, and avocado.
2. In another one, mix lime juice, olive oil, cumin, salt, and pepper.
3. Pour the dressing over the salad and toss to combine.
4. Serve or chill in the refrigerator before serving for enhanced flavors.

Nutritional Facts:
Calories: 310 | Protein: 8g | Carbohydrates: 38g | Fat: 15g | Fiber: 8g

Thai Basil Chicken

What do you need:

- 1 lb ground chicken
- 2 tablespoons GF soy sauce or tamari sauce
- 1 tablespoon fish sauce
- 1 tablespoon honey
- 1 bunch basil leaves, roughly torn
- 3 cloves garlic, minced
- 1 chili, sliced (optional)
- 2 tablespoons vegetable oil
- Salt to taste

How to Proceed:

1. Warm up oil in a large skillet over medium-high heat.
2. Mix garlic and chili, sauté for about 1 minute until fragrant.
3. Incorporate ground chicken, breaking it apart with a spatula, and sauté until cooked through, about 5-7 minutes.
4. Stir in soy sauce, fish sauce, and honey, and cook for an additional 2 minutes.
5. Remove from heat and stir in basil leaves until wilted.
6. Serve hot with a side of cooked rice or over lettuce wraps.

Nutritional Facts:
Calories: 280 | Protein: 23g | Carbohydrates: 10g | Fat: 16g | Fiber: 1g

Indian Spiced Chickpeas

What do you need:

- 1 can (15 oz) chickpeas, drained and rinsed
- 1 onion, finely chopped
- 2 teaspoons garam masala
- 1 teaspoon turmeric
- 1/2 teaspoon chili powder
- 2 tablespoons olive/vegetable oil
- Salt to taste
- Fresh cilantro, for garnish

How to Proceed:

1. Warm up oil in a skillet over medium heat.
2. Mix onion and sauté until translucent, about 3-4 minutes.
3. Incorporate garam masala, turmeric, and chili powder, and cook for 1 minute until spices are fragrant.
4. Stir in chickpeas and season with salt. Cook for about 5-7 minutes until chickpeas are heated through and coated with spices.
5. Garnish with fresh cilantro before serving.

Nutritional Facts: Calories: 250 | Protein: 9g | Carbohydrates: 30g | Fat: 10g | Fiber: 8g

Japanese Miso Soup

What do you need:

- 4 cups water
- 2 tablespoons GF miso paste
- 1/2 cup tofu, cubed
- 1/4 cup seaweed, chopped
- 2 green onions, chopped
- 1 teaspoon sesame oil

How to Proceed:

1. Bring water to a simmer in a pot.
2. Place miso paste in a small bowl, add a bit of hot water, and whisk until smooth.
3. Add the miso mixture back to the pot. Stir in tofu, seaweed, and most of the green onions. Simmer for about 3-5 minutes. Do not boil to preserve the probiotics in miso.
4. Remove from heat, stir in sesame oil, and garnish with remaining green onions.

Nutritional Facts: Calories: 80 | Protein: 5g | Carbohydrates: 7g | Fat: 4g | Fiber: 1g

Korean Beef Bowl

What do you need:

- 1 lb ground beef
- 1/4 cup GF soy sauce
- 2 tablespoons sesame oil
- 1 tablespoon sugar or honey
- 2 cloves garlic, minced
- 1 teaspoon grated ginger
- 1/4 teaspoon red pepper flakes
- 2 green onions, chopped
- 1 tablespoon sesame seeds
- Cooked rice for serving

How to Proceed:

1. Heat a large skillet over medium-high heat.
2. Add ground beef and cook until browned, breaking it up with a spoon, about 5-7 minutes.
3. Drain excess fat and return to heat.
4. Stir in soy sauce, sesame oil, sugar or honey, garlic, ginger, and red pepper flakes. Cook for another 2-3 minutes, stirring frequently.
5. Serve the beef over cooked rice, garnished with green onions and sesame seeds.

Nutritional Facts: Calories: 360 | Protein: 23g | Carbohydrates: 14g | Fat: 23g | Fiber: 1g

Greek Lemon Garlic Chicken Skewers

What do you need:

- 1 lb chicken breast, cut into cubes
- 3 tablespoons olive/vegetable oil
- Juice of 1 lemon
- 3 cloves garlic, minced
- 1 teaspoon dried oregano
- Salt and pepper to taste
- Fresh parsley, chopped for garnish
- Lemon wedges for serving

How to Proceed:

1. In a pot, mix oil, lemon juice, minced garlic, oregano, salt, and pepper.
2. Add the chicken cubes to the marinade and let sit for 5 minutes (or longer if time allows).
3. Thread the chicken onto skewers.
4. Heat a grill pan over medium-high heat. Grill the skewers, turning occasionally, until the chicken is golden brown and cooked through, about 10-12 minutes.
5. Garnish with chopped parsley and serve with lemon wedges on the side.

Nutritional Facts: Calories: 270 | Protein: 26g | Carbohydrates: 3g | Fat: 17g | Fiber: 0g

Moroccan Chickpea Soup

What do you need:

- 1 can (15 oz) chickpeas, drained and rinsed
- 2 cups hot GF vegetable broth
- 1 can (14.5 oz) diced tomatoes
- 1 onion, chopped
- 2 cloves garlic, minced
- 1 teaspoon cumin
- 1 teaspoon coriander
- 1/2 teaspoon cinnamon
- 2 tablespoons olive oil
- Salt and pepper to taste
- Fresh cilantro for garnish

How to Proceed:

1. Warm up oil in a large pot over medium heat.
2. Add onion and garlic and sauté until onion is translucent, about 5 minutes.
3. Stir in cumin, coriander, and cinnamon and cook for 1 minute until fragrant.
4. Incorporate chickpeas, diced tomatoes, and vegetable broth. Bring to a boil, then reduce heat and simmer for 10 minutes.
5. Season with salt and pepper to taste.
6. Garnish with fresh cilantro before serving.

Nutritional Facts: Calories: 220 | Protein: 8g | Carbohydrates: 30g | Fat: 8g | Fiber: 7g

Spanish Paella with Seafood

What do you need:

- 1 cup rice
- 2 cups hot seafood stock
- 1/2 lb mixed seafood (shrimp, scallops, mussels, cleaned and prepped)
- 1/2 cup peas
- 1 red bell pepper, sliced
- 1/2 onion, chopped
- 1 clove garlic, minced
- 1/2 teaspoon saffron threads
- 2 tablespoons olive oil
- Salt and pepper to taste
- Lemon wedges for serving

How to Proceed:

1. In a large skillet, warm up oil over medium heat.
2. Add onion, bell pepper, and garlic, and sauté until soft, about 5 minutes.
3. Stir in rice, saffron, and seafood stock. Bring to a boil.
4. Reduce heat to low and simmer for about 10 minutes.
5. Add the seafood and peas and cook until the seafood is cooked through and rice is tender, about 5 minutes.
6. Season with salt and pepper.
7. Serve hot with lemon wedges on the side.

Nutritional Facts:
Calories: 350 | Protein: 20g | Carbohydrates: 40g | Fat: 12g | Fiber: 1g

Japanese Miso Soup

What do you need:

- 4 cups water
- 2 tablespoons GF miso paste
- 1/2 cup tofu, cubed
- 1/4 cup seaweed, chopped
- 2 green onions, chopped
- 1 teaspoon sesame oil

How to Proceed:

8. Bring water to a simmer in a pot.
9. Place miso paste in a small bowl, add a bit of hot water, and whisk until smooth.
10. Add the miso mixture back to the pot. Stir in tofu, seaweed, and most of the green onions. Simmer for about 3-5 minutes. Do not boil to preserve the probiotics in miso.
11. Remove from heat, stir in sesame oil, and garnish with remaining green onions.

Nutritional Facts: Calories: 80 | Protein: 5g | Carbohydrates: 7g | Fat: 4g | Fiber: 1g

Mexican Guacamole Tostadas

What do you need:

- 4 GF corn tostadas
- 1 ripe avocado, mashed
- 1/4 cup diced red onion
- 1/4 cup diced tomatoes
- 1 tbsp lime juice
- 1/4 tsp cumin
- Salt and pepper to taste

How to Proceed:

1. In a bowl, mix mashed avocado, red onion, tomatoes, lime juice, cumin, salt, and pepper.
2. Spread the guacamole mixture evenly over each tostada.
3. Top with additional diced tomatoes or cilantro if desired.
4. Serve immediately.

Nutritional Facts: Calories: 150 | Protein: 2g | Carbohydrates: 18g | Fat: 9g | Fiber: 5g

Japanese Edamame and Seaweed Salad

What do you need:

- 1 cup cooked edamame (shelled)
- 1/4 cup rehydrated seaweed (wakame)
- 1 tbsp GF soy sauce or tamari
- 1 tbsp rice vinegar
- 1/2 tsp sesame oil
- 1 tsp sesame seeds

How to Proceed:

1. In a bowl, combine cooked edamame and rehydrated seaweed.
2. Drizzle with soy sauce, rice vinegar, and sesame oil.
3. Sprinkle with sesame seeds and toss gently to combine.
4. Serve immediately.

Nutritional Facts: Calories: 120 | Protein: 8g | Carbohydrates: 10g | Fat: 6g | Fiber: 3g

Indian Masala Chickpea Wrap

What do you need:

- 1 gluten-free tortilla
- 1/2 cup canned chickpeas, drained and rinsed
- 1/4 tsp ground turmeric
- 1/4 tsp ground cumin
- 1/4 tsp ground coriander
- 1/4 cup diced tomatoes
- 1 tbsp chopped cilantro
- 1 tbsp dairy-free yogurt (optional)

How to Proceed:

1. In a small bowl, mix chickpeas with turmeric, cumin, coriander, and a pinch of salt.
2. Warm the GF tortilla in a pan for 1 minute.
3. Spread the spiced chickpeas down the center of the tortilla.
4. Top with diced tomatoes, cilantro, and dairy-free yogurt if using.
5. Roll up the tortilla tightly and serve immediately.

Nutritional Facts: Calories: 180 | Protein: 6g | Carbohydrates: 26g | Fat: 5g | Fiber: 5g

Thai Spring Rolls

What do you need:

- 4 rice paper wrappers
- 1/4 cup cooked shrimp or tofu, sliced
- 1/4 cup rice vermicelli noodles, cooked
- 1/4 cup shredded lettuce
- 1/4 cup shredded carrots
- Fresh mint leaves
- 2 tbsp GF hoisin sauce for dipping

How to Proceed:

1. Dip each rice paper wrapper in warm water for about 10 seconds to soften.
2. Lay the softened wrapper on a flat surface.
3. Layer a small amount of shrimp or tofu, vermicelli noodles, lettuce, carrots, and mint leaves in the center.
4. Fold the sides of the wrapper over the filling, then roll it up tightly.
5. Serve immediately with GF hoisin sauce for dipping.

Nutritional Facts: Calories: 120 | Protein: 6g | Carbohydrates: 20g | Fat: 2g | Fiber: 2g

Egg-Free Fruit and Nut Parfait

What do you need:

- 1 cup dairy-free yogurt (such as coconut or almond yogurt)
- 1/2 cup mixed berries (blueberries, raspberries, strawberries)
- 2 tbsp GF granola
- 1 tbsp chopped nuts (like almonds or walnuts)
- 1 tsp honey or maple syrup (optional)

How to Proceed:

1. In a glass or bowl, layer half of the yogurt, then half of the mixed berries.
2. Sprinkle with 1 tablespoon of granola and some chopped nuts.
3. Repeat the layers with the remaining yogurt, berries, granola, and nuts.
4. Drizzle with honey or maple syrup if desired.
5. Serve immediately.

Nutritional Facts: Calories: 180 | Protein: 4g | Carbohydrates: 30g | Fat: 7g | Fiber: 4g

Italian Caponata Crostini

What do you need:

- 4 slices GF baguette or bread, toasted
- 1/2 cup store-bought caponata (eggplant relish)
- 1 tbsp chopped fresh basil
- 1 tbsp pine nuts (optional)

How to Proceed:

1. Spread a generous amount of caponata on each slice of toasted GF baguette.
2. Sprinkle with chopped fresh basil and pine nuts if using.
3. Arrange on a serving platter and serve immediately.

Nutritional Facts: Calories: 140 | Protein: 3g | Carbohydrates: 22g | Fat: 5g | Fiber: 3g

Moroccan Carrot Salad

What do you need:

- 1 cup shredded carrots
- 2 tbsp raisins
- 1 tbsp chopped fresh cilantro
- 1 tbsp lemon juice
- 1 tbsp olive oil
- 1/2 tsp ground cumin
- Salt and pepper to taste

How to Proceed:

1. In a bowl, combine shredded carrots, raisins, and chopped cilantro.
2. In a small bowl, whisk together lemon juice, olive oil, ground cumin, salt, and pepper.
3. Pour the dressing over the carrot mixture and toss to combine.
4. Serve immediately.

Nutritional Facts: Calories: 120 | Protein: 1g | Carbohydrates: 15g | Fat: 7g | Fiber: 3g

SNACKS AND APPETIZERS

Here are several quick and easy gluten-free snack and appetizer recipes that you can whip up in 15 minutes or less, perfect for satisfying hunger between meals or for serving at gatherings.

Roasted Chickpeas

What do you need (Serves 4):

- 1 can (15 oz) chickpeas, rinsed and drained
- 1 tablespoon olive/vegetable oil
- 1/2 teaspoon smoked paprika
- 1/2 teaspoon garlic powder
- Salt to taste

How to Proceed:

1. Preheat your oven to 400°F (200°C).
2. Pat the chickpeas dry with paper towels, removing any skins that come off.
3. Toss the chickpeas with olive oil, smoked paprika, garlic powder, and salt.
4. Spread the chickpeas on a baking sheet in a single layer.
5. Roast in the oven for about 10-12 minutes, or until crispy and golden.
6. Let cool slightly before serving as they become crisper as they cool.

Nutritional Facts:
Calories: 150 | Protein: 6g | Carbohydrates: 20g | Fat: 5g | Fiber: 6g

Kale Chips

What do you need (Serves 4):

- 1 bunch kale, washed, dried, and torn into bite-size pieces
- 1 tablespoon olive oil
- Salt to taste

How to Proceed:

1. Warm up your oven to 350°F (175°C).
2. Toss kale pieces with olive oil and salt in a large bowl.
3. Spread the kale in a single layer on a baking sheet.
4. Bake in the oven for about 10-12 minutes, or until the edges are brown but not burnt.
5. Serve immediately for the crispiest texture.

Nutritional Facts: Calories: 60 | Protein: 2g | Carbohydrates: 5g | Fat: 4g | Fiber: 1g

Crackers with Cheese Spread

What do you need:

- 1 box GF crackers
- 1 cup dairy-free cheese spread (check it's gluten-free)

How to Proceed:

1. Arrange the GF crackers on a serving plate.
2. Place the dairy-free cheese spread in a small bowl alongside the crackers.
3. Guests or family members can spread their own crackers as they enjoy.

Nutritional Facts: Calories: 200 | Protein: 3g | Carbohydrates: 20g | Fat: 12g | Fiber: 2g

Garlic Mashed Potatoes

What do you need (Serve 4):

- 4 medium potatoes, peeled and cubed
- 2 cloves garlic, minced
- 1/4 cup milk or almond milk (dairy-free option)
- 2 tablespoons butter or olive oil (dairy-free option)
- Salt and pepper to taste

How to Proceed:

1. Place potatoes in a medium pot and cover with water. Bring to a boil and cook until tender, about 10-12 minutes.
2. Drain the potatoes and return them to the pot.
3. Incorporate the minced garlic, milk, and butter or oil to the potatoes.
4. Mash the potatoes until smooth and creamy.
5. Serve warm.

Nutritional Facts:
Calories: 200 | Protein: 4g | Carbohydrates: 35g | Fat: 5g | Fiber: 4g

Stuffed Dates

What do you need:

- 12 Medjool dates, pitted
- 1/2 cup almond butter/mascarpone
- 1/4 cup crushed almonds or pecans
- A pinch of sea salt

How to Proceed:

1. Slit each date on one side to create an opening.
2. Fill each date with about a teaspoon of almond butter.
3. Press some crushed nuts into the almond butter.
4. Sprinkle a tiny pinch of sea salt on each stuffed date.
5. Serve immediately or chill for a firmer texture.

Nutritional Facts:
Calories: 140 (per date)| Protein: 2g | Carbohydrates: 18g | Fat: 7g | Fiber: 1g

Deviled Avocado Eggs (Egg-Free Version)

What do you need:

- 2 ripe avocados
- 1 tbsp lime juice
- 1 clove garlic, minced
- 1/4 tsp cumin
- 1/4 tsp paprika
- Salt and pepper to taste
- Optional: chopped chives or cilantro for garnish

How to Proceed:

1. Cut the avocados in half and remove the pits.
2. Scoop out some of the flesh, leaving a small border, and place it in a bowl.
3. Mash the avocado flesh with lime juice, garlic, cumin, paprika, salt, and pepper.
4. Spoon the mashed avocado back into the avocado halves.
5. Garnish with chopped chives or cilantro if desired.
6. Serve immediately.

Nutritional Facts: Calories: 160 | Protein: 2g | Carbohydrates: 9g | Fat: 15g | Fiber: 7g

Zucchini Fritters

What do you need:

- 1 medium zucchini, grated
- 1/4 cup GF flour blend
- 1 tbsp chopped fresh parsley
- 1 clove garlic, minced
- Salt and pepper to taste
- 1 tbsp olive oil for frying

How to Proceed:

1. Place grated zucchini in a clean kitchen towel and squeeze out excess moisture.
2. In a bowl, combine zucchini, GF flour, parsley, garlic, salt, and pepper.
3. Heat olive oil in a skillet over medium heat.
4. Drop spoonfuls of the zucchini mixture into the skillet, flattening them slightly with a spatula.
5. Fry for 2-3 minutes on each side until golden brown.
6. Serve immediately.

Nutritional Facts: Calories: 120 | Protein: 2g | Carbohydrates: 15g | Fat: 7g | Fiber: 2g

Cheesy Spinach Dip

What do you need:

- 1 cup fresh spinach, chopped
- 1/2 cup dairy-free cream cheese
- 1/4 cup dairy-free shredded mozzarella cheese
- 1 clove garlic, minced
- Salt and pepper to taste
- GF crackers or veggie sticks for dipping

How to Proceed:

1. In a microwave-safe bowl, combine chopped spinach, dairy-free cream cheese, shredded mozzarella, and minced garlic.
2. Microwave on high for 1-2 minutes until the cheese is melted and the mixture is heated through.
3. Stir well and season with salt and pepper to taste.
4. Serve immediately with GF crackers or veggie sticks.

Nutritional Facts: Calories: 150 | Protein: 3g | Carbohydrates: 8g | Fat: 12g | Fiber: 2g

Apple and Almond Butter Sandwiches

What do you need:

- 1 apple, cored and sliced into rings
- 2 tbsp almond butter
- 1 tbsp GF granola (optional)
- 1 tsp honey (optional)

How to Proceed:

1. Spread almond butter on half of the apple slices.
2. Sprinkle with GF granola if using.
3. Top with the remaining apple slices to create a sandwich.
4. Drizzle with honey if desired.
5. Serve immediately.

Nutritional Facts: Calories: 120 | Protein: 2g | Carbohydrates: 18g | Fat: 6g | Fiber: 3g

Turkey and Veggie Roll-Ups

What do you need:

- 4 slices GF deli turkey
- 1/4 cup shredded carrots
- 1/4 cup sliced cucumber
- 1/4 cup baby spinach leaves
- 1 tbsp hummus or mustard (optional)

How to Proceed:

1. Lay out the turkey slices on a flat surface.
2. Spread a thin layer of hummus or mustard on each slice if desired.
3. Place shredded carrots, sliced cucumber, and spinach leaves on top of each turkey slice.
4. Roll up tightly and secure with a toothpick if needed. Serve immediately.

Nutritional Facts: Calories: 100 | Protein: 10g | Carbohydrates: 5g | Fat: 4g | Fiber: 1g

DESSERTS AND SWEET TREATS

Whip up these quick and delicious gluten-free desserts and sweet treats in 15 minutes or less. Whether you're craving something chocolaty, fruity, or creamy, these recipes ensure a satisfying finish to any meal or a delightful snack at any time of the day.

Chocolate Avocado Mousse

What do you need:

- 2 ripe avocados, peeled and pitted
- 1/4 cup cocoa powder
- 1/4 cup honey or maple syrup
- 1 teaspoon vanilla extract
- Pinch of salt
- Fresh raspberries or mint for garnish (optional)

How to Proceed:

1. In a blender or food processor, combine avocados, cocoa powder, honey (or maple syrup), vanilla extract, and salt.
2. Blend until smooth and creamy, scraping down the sides as needed.
3. Spoon the mousse into serving dishes and refrigerate for about 10 minutes to set slightly.
4. Garnish with fresh raspberries or a sprig of mint before serving.

Nutritional Facts: Calories: 240 | Protein: 3g | Carbohydrates: 30g | Fat: 15g | Fiber: 7g

Coconut Milk Ice Cream

What do you need:

- 1 can (14 oz) full-fat coconut milk
- 1/4 cup honey or maple syrup
- 1 teaspoon vanilla extract
- Pinch of salt

How to Proceed:

1. In a large bowl, whisk together coconut milk, honey (or maple syrup), vanilla extract, and salt.
2. Pour the mixture into an ice cream maker and churn according to the manufacturer's instructions until it reaches a soft-serve consistency, usually about 10-15 minutes.
3. Serve immediately for soft serve or transfer to a freezer-safe container and freeze for a few hours for a firmer texture.

Nutritional Facts:
Calories: 180 | Protein: 2g | Carbohydrates: 20g | Fat: 12g | Fiber: 1g

Dairy-Free Cheesecake Bites

What do you need:

- 1 cup cashews, soaked for 4 hours then drained
- 1/4 cup coconut/vegetable oil, melted
- 1/4 cup lemon juice
- 1/4 cup honey or maple syrup
- 1 teaspoon vanilla extract
- Pinch of salt
- Fresh berries for topping

How to Proceed:

1. In a food processor, blend cashews, coconut oil, lemon juice, honey (or maple syrup), vanilla extract, and salt until very smooth.
2. Spoon the mixture into mini muffin tins lined with paper or silicone liners.
3. Freeze for about 10 minutes until set.
4. Top with fresh berries before serving.

Nutritional Facts:
Calories: 150 | Protein: 3g | Carbohydrates: 10g | Fat: 12g | Fiber: 1g

Fruit Sorbet

What do you need:
- 2 cups frozen fruit (such as strawberries, mango, or peach)
- 1/4 cup honey or maple syrup
- 2 tablespoons lemon juice

How to Proceed:
1. In a food processor or high-powered blender, blend the frozen fruit, honey (or maple syrup), and lemon juice until smooth.
2. Serve immediately for a soft texture or freeze for a few hours for a firmer sorbet.

Nutritional Facts:
Calories: 120 | Protein: 1g | Carbohydrates: 30g | Fat: 0g | Fiber: 1g

Almond Butter Cookies

What do you need:

- 1 cup almond butter
- 1/2 cup coconut sugar
- 1 egg (use a flax egg for vegan version: 1 tbsp ground flaxseed mixed with 3 tbsp water)
- 1 teaspoon vanilla extract
- 1/2 teaspoon baking soda
- Pinch of salt

How to Proceed:

1. Preheat oven to 350°F (175°C).
2. In a bowl, mix almond butter, coconut sugar, egg (or flax egg), vanilla extract, baking soda, and salt until well combined.
3. Drop spoonfuls of the dough onto a parchment-lined baking sheet.
4. Bake for 8-10 minutes, or until the edges are slightly golden.
5. Let cool on the baking sheet for a few minutes before transferring to a wire rack.

Nutritional Facts:
Calories: 140 | Protein: 4g | Carbohydrates: 10g | Fat: 12g | Fiber: 2g

Lemon Bars

What do you need:

- 1 cup almond flour
- 1/4 cup coconut oil, melted
- 2 tablespoons honey (for the crust)
- Pinch of salt

For the filling:
- ✓ 2 eggs
- ✓ 1/2 cup fresh lemon juice
- ✓ 1/4 cup honey
- ✓ 2 tablespoons GF cornstarch

How to Proceed:

1. Preheat your oven to 350°F (175°C).
2. Mix almond flour, melted coconut oil, 2 tablespoons of honey, and a pinch of salt in a bowl. Press the mixture into the bottom of a lined 8x8 inch baking dish.
3. Bake the crust for about 10 minutes, or until just golden.
4. While the crust is baking, whisk together eggs, lemon juice, 1/4 cup honey, and cornstarch until smooth.
5. Pour the lemon mixture over the hot crust.
6. Bake for another 12-15 minutes, or until the filling is set.
7. Cool completely before cutting into bars. Refrigerate to firm up more if desired.

Nutritional Facts:
Calories: 180 | Protein: 4g | Carbohydrates: 16g | Fat: 12g | Fiber: 1g

Coconut Macaroons

What do you need:

- 2 cups shredded coconut
- 3 egg whites
- 1/4 cup honey
- 1 teaspoon vanilla extract
- Pinch of salt

How to Proceed:

1. Preheat your oven to 325°F (165°C).
2. In a bowl, whisk together egg whites, honey, vanilla extract, and a pinch of salt until well combined.
3. Stir in the shredded coconut until the mixture is well coated.
4. Drop spoonfuls of the mixture onto a parchment-lined baking sheet.
5. Bake for 12-15 minutes, or until the edges are golden brown.
6. Let cool on the baking sheet before transferring to a rack to cool completely.

Nutritional Facts:
Calories: 100 | Protein: 2g | Carbohydrates: 9g | Fat: 7g | Fiber: 1g

Quick Peanut Butter Cookies

What do you need:

- 1 cup GF peanut butter
- 1 cup sugar
- 1 egg
- 1 teaspoon vanilla extract

How to Proceed:

1. Warm up your oven to 350°F (175°C).
2. In a bowl, mix peanut butter, sugar, egg, and vanilla extract until well combined.
3. Roll the dough into 1-inch balls and place on a parchment-lined baking sheet. Press down with a fork to create a criss-cross pattern.
4. Bake for 8-10 minutes or until the edges are slightly golden.
5. Let cool on the baking sheet for a few minutes before transferring to a cooling rack.

Nutritional Facts: Calories: 190 | Protein: 4g | Carbohydrates: 18g | Fat: 12g | Fiber: 1g

Flourless Chocolate Cake

What do you need:

- 1 cup GF semisweet chocolate chips
- 1/2 cup unsalted butter
- 3/4 cup granulated sugar
- 1/4 teaspoon salt
- 1 teaspoon vanilla extract
- 3 eggs
- 1/2 cup unsweetened cocoa powder

How to Proceed:

1. Preheat your oven to 375°F (190°C).
2. In a microwave-safe bowl, combine chocolate chips and butter. Microwave in 30-second intervals, stirring in between, until completely melted and smooth.
3. Stir in sugar, salt, and vanilla extract.
4. Add eggs one at a time, whisking well after each addition.
5. Sift cocoa powder over the mixture and fold it in until just combined.
6. Pour the batter into a greased 8-inch cake pan.
7. Bake for 20-25 minutes or until the top has formed a thin crust.
8. Cool in the pan on a wire rack before serving.

Nutritional Facts:
Calories: 320 | Protein: 5g | Carbohydrates: 34g | Fat: 20g | Fiber: 1g

Almond Flour Biscuits

What do you need:

- 2 cups almond flour
- 1 tsp GF baking powder
- 1/4 tsp salt
- 2 tbsp cold butter, diced
- 2 eggs
- 1/3 cup almond milk or any kind of milk

How to Proceed:

1. Warm up the oven to 350°F (175°C) and line a baking sheet with parchment paper.
2. In a pot, mix almond flour, baking powder, and salt. Cut in the butter until the mixture resembles coarse crumbs.
3. In another bowl, mix the eggs with almond milk, then stir into the dry ingredients until the dough comes together.
4. Drop spoonfuls of the dough onto the baking sheet.
5. Bake for 12-15 minutes, or until the biscuits are golden and firm.
6. Serve warm.

Nutritional Facts:

Calories: 160 | Protein: 6g | Carbohydrates: 6g | Fat: 14g | Fiber: 3g

Cornbread Muffins

What do you need (Serve 12):

- 1 cup GF cornmeal
- 1/2 cup GF all-purpose flour
- 2 tsp GF baking powder
- 1/4 tsp salt
- 1/4 cup honey or maple syrup
- 1 cup almond milk
- 1/4 cup vegetable oil
- 1 egg

How to Proceed:

1. Warm up the oven to 375°F (190°C) and grease or line a muffin pan with paper liners.
2. In a pot, mix cornmeal, flour, baking powder, and salt.
3. In another one, incorporate almond milk, oil, egg, and honey.
4. Combine the wet and dry ingredients until just mixed. Do not overmix.
5. Spoon the batter into the prepared muffin pan, filling each cup about two-thirds full.
6. Bake for 15-18 minutes, or until a toothpick check is ok.
7. Let cool slightly before serving.

Nutritional Facts:

Calories: 180 | Protein: 3g | Carbohydrates: 28g | Fat: 7g | Fiber: 2g

SAUCES, DRESSINGS, AND STAPLES

Enhance your meals with these quick and easy gluten-free sauces and dressings. Each can be whipped up in under 15 minutes, perfect for adding extra flavor to any dish.
COOKING TIP: these sauces and dressings can be prepared in advance or in larger quantities because they will keep for up to a week in the refrigerator if stored in airtight containers.

Peanut Sauce

What do you need:

- 1/2 cup GF peanut butter (smooth or crunchy)
- 2 tablespoons GF soy sauce
- 2 tablespoons honey or maple syrup
- 1 tablespoon lime juice
- 1 teaspoon grated ginger
- 1 clove garlic, minced
- Water to thin (as needed)

How to Proceed:

1. In a small bowl, whisk together peanut butter, soy sauce, honey (or maple syrup), lime juice, ginger, and garlic until smooth.
2. Gradually add water a tablespoon at a time until desired consistency is reached.
3. Taste and adjust seasoning, adding more lime juice or honey if desired.
4. Serve as a dip or dressing, or over noodles or salad.

Nutritional Facts:
Calories: 150 (serving size 2 tablespoons) | Protein: 4g | Carbohydrates: 9g | Fat: 12g | Fiber: 1g

Pesto Sauce

What do you need:

- 2 cups fresh basil leaves
- 1/2 cup grated GF Parmesan cheese or similar
- 1/3 cup pine nuts
- 2 cloves garlic
- 1/2 cup olive/vegetable oil
- Salt and pepper to taste

How to Proceed:

1. In a food processor, combine basil, Parmesan cheese, pine nuts, and garlic.
2. Pulse while gradually adding the olive oil until the mixture forms a smooth paste.
3. Season with salt and pepper to taste.
4. Use immediately over pasta, as a spread, or store in the refrigerator.

Nutritional Facts:
Calories: 180 per serving (serving size 2 tablespoons) | Protein: 3g | Carbohydrates: 1g | Fat: 18g | Fiber: 0g

Teriyaki Sauce

What do you need:

- 1/2 cup GF soy sauce
- 1/4 cup water
- 2 tablespoons brown sugar
- 1 tablespoon honey
- 2 cloves garlic, minced
- 1 teaspoon grated ginger
- 1 tablespoon cornstarch mixed with 1 tablespoon water (slurry)

How to Proceed:

1. In a small saucepan, combine soy sauce, water, brown sugar, honey, garlic, and ginger.
2. Bring to a simmer over medium heat.
3. Add the cornstarch slurry and stir continuously until the sauce thickens, about 2-3 minutes.
4. Remove from heat and let cool slightly before using, or store in the refrigerator for later use.

Nutritional Facts:
Calories: 50 (serving size 1 tablespoon)| Protein: 1g | Carbohydrates: 10g | Fat: 0g | Fiber: 0g

Balsamic Vinaigrette

What do you need:

- 1/4 cup balsamic vinegar
- 1/2 cup olive/vegetable oil
- 1 teaspoon GF mustard
- 1 clove garlic, minced
- Salt and pepper to taste

How to Proceed:

1. In a jar with a tight-fitting lid, combine balsamic vinegar, olive oil, mustard, and minced garlic.
2. Close the lid tightly and shake vigorously until well combined.
3. Season with salt and pepper to taste.
4. Serve over salads or as a marinade for meats and vegetables.

Nutritional Facts:
Calories: 120 (serving size 1 tablespoon)| Protein: 0g | Carbohydrates: 1g | Fat: 12g | Fiber: 0g

Caesar Dressing

What do you need:

- 1/2 cup GF mayonnaise
- 1/4 cup grated Parmesan cheese
- 2 cloves garlic, minced
- 2 tablespoons lemon juice
- 1 teaspoon GF mustard
- 1 teaspoon GF Worcestershire sauce
- 1/4 teaspoon black pepper
- Anchovy paste to taste (optional)

How to Proceed:

1. In a bowl, whisk together mayonnaise, Parmesan cheese, garlic, lemon juice, mustard, Worcestershire sauce, and black pepper until smooth.
2. Add a small amount of anchovy paste if desired, and whisk until fully incorporated.
3. Adjust seasoning to taste. Store in the refrigerator until ready to use.

Nutritional Facts:
Calories: 110 | Protein: 2g | Carbohydrates: 1g | Fat: 11g | Fiber: 0g

Chimichurri Sauce

What do you need:

- 1 cup fresh parsley, finely chopped
- 1/4 cup fresh oregano, finely chopped
- 3 cloves garlic, minced
- 1/2 cup olive/vegetable oil
- 2 tablespoons red wine vinegar
- 1 teaspoon red pepper flakes
- Salt and pepper to taste

How to Proceed:

1. In a bowl, mix together parsley, oregano, garlic, olive oil, red wine vinegar, and red pepper flakes.
2. Season with salt and pepper to taste.
3. Let sit for at least 10 minutes to allow flavors to meld before serving.
4. Store in the refrigerator for up to a week or serve immediately over grilled meats or vegetables.

Nutritional Facts: Calories: 120 (serving size 1 tablespoon) | Protein: 0g | Carbohydrates: 1g | Fat: 12g | Fiber: 1g

Honey Mustard Dressing

What do you need:

- 1/3 cup GF mayonnaise
- 1/4 cup GF mustard
- 1/4 cup honey
- 1 tablespoon apple cider vinegar
- Salt and pepper to taste

How to Proceed:

1. In a small bowl, whisk together mayonnaise, mustard, honey, and apple cider vinegar until smooth.
2. Season with salt and pepper to taste.
3. Store in an airtight container in the refrigerator until ready to use.

Nutritional Facts: Calories: 80 (serving size 1 tablespoon) | Protein: 0g | Carbohydrates: 8g | Fat: 5g | Fiber: 0g

Ranch Dressing

What do you need:

- 1/2 cup GF mayonnaise
- 1/2 cup GF sour cream (or dairy-free alternative)
- 1 teaspoon dried chives
- 1 teaspoon dried parsley
- 1 teaspoon dried dill
- 1/2 teaspoon garlic powder
- 1/2 teaspoon onion powder
- 1 tablespoon lemon juice
- Salt and pepper to taste

How to Proceed:

1. In a bowl, whisk together mayonnaise, sour cream, chives, parsley, dill, garlic powder, onion powder, and lemon juice until smooth.
2. Season with salt and pepper to taste.
3. Refrigerate for at least 30 minutes before serving to let flavors develop.
4. Use as a dressing for salads or as a dip for vegetables.

Nutritional Facts:
Calories: 100 | Protein: 1g | Carbohydrates: 2g | Fat: 10g | Fiber: 0g

Quick Marinara Sauce

What do you need:

- 1 can (14 oz) crushed tomatoes
- 2 cloves garlic, minced
- 1 tablespoon olive oil
- 1 teaspoon dried basil
- 1 teaspoon dried oregano
- Salt and pepper to taste

How to Proceed:

1. Warm up oil in a saucepan over medium heat.
2. Add minced garlic and sauté for about 1 minute until fragrant.
3. Pour in the crushed tomatoes, basil, oregano, salt, and pepper.
4. Simmer for about 10 minutes, stirring occasionally.
5. Adjust seasoning as needed and use immediately or store in the refrigerator for later use.

Nutritional Facts:
Calories: 35 (serving size 1/4 cup)| Protein: 1g | Carbohydrates: 4g | Fat: 2g | Fiber: 1g

FOOD LIST

GRAINS AND FLOURS

- Rice
- Corn
- Millet
- Quinoa
- Buckwheat
- Amaranth
- Teff
- Sorghum
- Potatoes
- Rice flour
- Corn flour
- Buckwheat flour
- Tapioca flour
- Chickpea flour
- Chestnut flour
- Almond flour
- Cornstarch
- Potato starch

BREAD, PASTA, AND BAKED GOODS

- Gluten-free bread
- Rice pasta
- Corn pasta
- Buckwheat pasta
- Rice cakes
- Rice crackers
- Gluten-free cookies
- Gluten-free pizza
- Gluten-free cakes and pastries

DAIRY/ DIARY PRODUCTS

- Milk
- Plain yogurt
- Butter
- Cream
- Cheese

LEGUMES

- Lentils
- Beans
- Chickpeas
- Peas
- Soybeans
- Fava beans

MEAT, FISH, AND EGGS

- All types of fresh meat and fish
- Eggs

FRUITS AND VEGETABLES

- All fresh fruits & fresh vegetables
- Vegetables in oil
- Potatoes

SEEDS AND OILS

- Sunflower seeds
- Pumpkin seeds
- Walnuts/nuts
- Almonds
- Pistachios
- Hazelnuts
- Flaxseeds
- Chia seeds
- Olive/seeds oil
- Vinegar
- Honey/sugar
- Dark Chocolate

Tips to Plan Sustainable Meals

Quick Prep Strategies for Weeknight Dinners

1. **Choose Fast Recipes:**
    - Focus on meals that require minimal prep and cook time
    - Opt for stir-fries, salads, and sheet-pan meals (under 30 minutes)

2. **Prep Ingredients in Advance:**
    - Chop vegetables, marinate proteins, pre-cook grains
    - Store prepped items in the refrigerator for easy access

3. **Stock Quick-cooking Staples:**
    - Keep canned beans, frozen vegetables, and gluten-free pasta on hand
    - Use these for quick, versatile meal options

4. **Batch Cooking:**
    - Prepare large quantities of food for the week ahead
    - Focus on soups, stews, casseroles, and grain-based salads
    - Cook basic components (e.g., chicken, quinoa, roasted vegetables) for mix-and-match meals

5. **Utilize Frozen and Pre-Cut Ingredients:**
    - Use frozen vegetables for convenience and long shelf life
    - Opt for pre-cut fresh vegetables to save time
    - Consider pre-cooked gluten-free grains and proteins

6. **Plan and Portion:**
    - Spend time on weekends cooking and portioning meals
    - Store individual servings for easy reheating during the week

By implementing these strategies, you can significantly reduce weeknight dinner stress, save time, and ensure you always have nutritious, gluten-free meals ready to go. This approach helps maintain a balanced diet while accommodating a busy schedule.

Planning for Success: How to Make Time-Saving a Habit

The key to consistently preparing quick and easy gluten-free meals lies in making time-saving strategies a regular part of your routine. Here are a few tips to help you build these habits:

Plan Your Meals Ahead: Set aside time each week to plan your meals. Decide what you'll cook each day, make a shopping list, and stick to it. Knowing what's for dinner ahead of time eliminates the stress of last-minute decision-making and ensures you have all the ingredients on hand.

Keep a List of Go-To Recipes: Compile a list of your favorite quick and easy gluten-free recipes. These should be meals that you can prepare in 30 minutes or less and that you know your family will enjoy. Having a go-to list makes meal planning faster and helps you avoid the overwhelm of choosing recipes from scratch each week.

Double Up When Cooking: Whenever you cook a meal that stores well, make a double batch. Eat one portion for dinner and save the other for a future meal. This strategy is particularly useful for dishes like soups, stews, and casseroles, which often taste even better the next day.

Organize Your Kitchen: A well-organized kitchen can dramatically speed up your cooking process. Keep your most-used tools and ingredients within easy reach, and store similar items together. For example, keep all your gluten-free flours and baking supplies in one area, and store your cooking oils and spices near the stove. The less time you spend searching for ingredients and tools, the faster you can get meals on the table.

Embrace Simplicity: Finally, remember that meals don't have to be complicated to be delicious and satisfying. Focus on simple, whole foods, and let the natural flavors of your ingredients shine. A simple grilled chicken breast with roasted vegetables and a side of quinoa can be just as enjoyable as a more elaborate dish—and it's much quicker to prepare.

By incorporating these time-saving tips into your routine, you can streamline your gluten-free meal preparation, making it easier to enjoy healthy, delicious meals even on your busiest days.

Supplementary Contents

Unlock Hidden Insights!

Scan the QR code below to access exclusive resources that complement your health journey through "15-Minute Gluten-free Cookbook for Beginners." I've included three carefully prepared bonus guides packed with valuable information and tips to help you manage your gluten-free lifestyle. I hope you find them helpful!

If you experience any problems or have feedback, contact us directly at **info@amazing-editions.com**. Your insights and experiences are crucial to our goal of providing the best guidance and support to our readers.

Made in United States
Cleveland, OH
26 December 2024

12637483R00042